THE EXPERIMENT

BECAUSE EVERY BOOK IS A TEST OF NEW IDEAS

Artisanal GLUTEN-FREE cupcakes

50 From-Scratch

Recipes to Delight

Every Cupcake Devotee—

Gluten-Free

and Otherwise

KELLI AND PETER BRONSKI

THE EXPERIMENT
NEW YORK

To our daughter, Charlotte

The Experiment, LLC
260 Fifth Avenue
New York, NY 10001-6408
www.theexperimentpublishing.com

The Experiment's books are available at special discounts when purchased in bulk for premiums and sales promotions, as well as for fundraising or educational use. For details, contact us at info@theexperimentpublishing.com.

Artisanal Gluten-Free Cupcakes includes a variety of gluten-free recipes as well as refined-sugar-free, dairy-free, egg-free, and vegan alternatives. While care was taken to provide correct and helpful information, the suggestions in this book are not intended as dietary advice or as a substitute for consulting a dietician or medical professional. We strongly recommend that you check with your doctor before making changes to your diet. The author and publisher disclaim all liability in connection with the use of this book.

Library of Congress Control Number: 2011925095

ISBN 978-1-61519-036-2
Ebook ISBN 978-1-61519-136-9

Cover design by Susi Oberhelman
Cover photographs by Kelli and Peter Bronski
Author photograph by Maury Wahtera
Text design by Pauline Neuwirth, Neuwirth & Associates, Inc.

Manufactured in Canada
Distributed by Workman Publishing Company, Inc.
Distributed simultaneously in Canada by Thomas Allen & Son Limited
First published June 2011

10 9 8 7 6 5 4 3 2 1

contents

preface

WHY AN ENTIRE cookbook dedicated to nothing but gluten-free cupcakes? For us, the answer comes down to a single word: *fun*. Cupcakes embody single-serving-size gluten-free baked goodness. In our opinion, there's a lot to love about them.

For one, they're great for portion control. When it comes to cupcakes, there's no question of "Did I cut the cake slices too thin or too thick?" Cupcakes are pre-portioned and ready to eat. Their small, single-person serving size also makes them satisfying. It's easy to finish off one cupcake in its entirety when you're left with nothing but the crumb-filled wrapper as evidence of your cupcake-consuming victory.

Speaking of the wrapper, we also love that cupcakes are basically finger food. Usually (though there *are* exceptions) there's no need for plates and forks. You simply grab a cupcake and go.

Cupcakes are also wonderfully versatile. Depending on the flavor combinations, decoration, and presentation, cupcakes can serve equally well for anytime snacking, children's parties, birthdays and other special occasions, and even weddings. Like the Little Black Dress that can be toned down and casual or dressed up and elegant, cupcakes can be anything from informal to formal (or somewhere in between).

Oh, and have we mentioned that cupcakes are simply delicious?

Finally, cupcakes are accessible. Honestly, it's hard to be intimidated by a cupcake, which is why novice bakers often gravitate toward them. Then again, so do experienced bakers, who perhaps go for more elaborate flavor combinations and more intricate or advanced decorations. The beauty of the cupcake, though, is that, at the end of the day, everyone's made the same thing—a tasty little tiny cake baked in the paper-lined cups of a tin tray.

There's no reason the gluten-free community can't have that same kind of cupcake satisfaction.

If you're holding this book and taking the time to read this preface, then the basic details of gluten-free living will likely be at least a little familiar to you. Gluten is a family of proteins found in wheat, barley, and rye. It causes a variety of serious health problems for people with conditions such as celiac disease, gluten intolerance, and wheat allergy. A gluten-free diet is the solution, and those of us in the gluten-free community are like everyone else in the sweet-loving world. We want to bake our cupcake and eat it, too. That's where this book comes in.

We hope this book becomes your go-to resource for fabulous gluten-free cupcakes.

In fact, we're so excited about these recipes—and confident of the results—we're willing to bet that if you don't tell them, your family and friends will never know these cupcakes are gluten-free. When Pete brought a batch of gluten-free Mocha Cupcakes (page 143) to a gluten-ous holiday party in the Poughkeepsie, New York, area, one person declared that the cupcakes were as delicious and decadent as anything she'd had from the nearby Culinary Institute of America. It was a small bit of flattering praise (and one we'll gladly accept!).

But you don't have to take our word for it. Try these recipes and see for yourself.

—*Kelli and Peter Bronski*, 2011

PART ONE

GET READY!

what is an *artisanal* gluten-free cupcake, anyway?

*A*rtisan is a term that often refers to the craft of hand-making certain food products. You've likely heard it used with references to artisan breads and artisan cheeses, especially. For us it's about more than just hand-making something. When it comes to gluten-free baking—and gluten-free cupcakes—the artisanal approach has a very specific meaning.

First, it involves baking with traditional, familiar ingredients, the kind you're likely to find in grocery stores and kitchen pantries across America. And it involves a preference for natural ingredients over artificial or imitation versions. For example, we use granulated sugar rather than an artificial sweetener such as Splenda, pure vanilla and other extracts and oils rather than imitation flavorings, and real butter rather than margarine.

Second, it emphasizes from-scratch methods of baking. You won't find any box cake mixes here! We build our recipes from the ground up, often opting to make ingredients or recipe components ourselves, like almond paste, dulce de leche, apple glaze, whipped cream—you name it.

Third, it uses classic techniques. From preparing an Italian buttercream to making a proper sponge cake, we don't take shortcuts. We make them as you'd learn to make them in culinary school or a pastry class, tweaked to adapt the techniques to the nuances of gluten-free baking. (Not that these classic techniques are difficult to do. None of the methods, techniques, and recipes in this book are beyond your reach. Trust us. You can do it, and do it well!)

The traditional ingredients, from-scratch recipes, and classic techniques all boil down to authenticity, although it might seem funny to call gluten-free recipes authentic. After all, the recipes might rightly be considered progressive rather than traditional, unconventional as opposed to conventional. Recipes usually made with wheat flour and other gluten-containing ingredients are updated for the present-day needs of the gluten-free community (as our guidelines for refined-sugar-free, dairy-free, and egg-free baking similarly do for those diet-restricted communities).

Then again, our recipes and our artisanal approach to gluten-free baking hark back to the way our grandmothers and great-grandmothers used to bake. Sure, they probably never heard of gluten, and they'd be even more shocked than we were initially getting up to speed on the ins and outs of the gluten-free diet. But we firmly believe that if they had a chance to see us at work in the kitchen, they'd recognize most of the ingredients, see us using the same techniques they once did, and, on the whole, approve of what we are doing.

And although a kind of posthumous approval from our baking ancestors is important to us, there are other reasons why we favor the artisanal approach as well. For one, it pays homage to different cultures and their food traditions. In a way the recipes on the pages of this book give a

Crumb Cake Cupcakes, *page 181*

nod to the pastries of France, the cannoli of Italy, the dulce de leche of Latin America.

This approach also gives a more absolute control of ingredients. There's little question as to the gluten-free status of an ingredient when you've made it yourself. (Almond paste is a perfect case in point: Some companies make a version that contains little more than almonds and sugar, but others make a version that includes wheat.)

We also believe that the artisanal approach often yields a healthier way to eat (at the very least by avoiding many of the artificial foods, ingredients, and additives that have been shown to be so bad for us). That's not to say, though, that eating an artisanal gluten-free cupcake is the dietary equivalent of a fresh salad. We are baking desserts here, after all. Cupcakes are a delightful indulgence, not an everyday health food.

Finally, our artisanal approach to gluten-free baking is simply a personal preference. We're old-fashioned romantics who value the time we spend together in the kitchen, the more intimate connection this approach gives us to the food we eat, and the opportunity it offers us to pass these recipes, ingredients, and techniques along to our daughters so they become the inheritors of an artisanal culinary legacy that started long before we used the word *artisanal* in the title of a book about cupcakes.

But enough waxing poetic. We're getting off our soapbox. We understand that ultimately there are probably only two questions that matter most to you: Are the recipes safely gluten-free, and how do the cupcakes taste?

We're firm believers that the artisanal approach delivers the best answers for both questions: Yes they are, and darned good!

why gluten-free?

Cupcakes are one thing. *Artisanal* cupcakes are another. But artisanal *gluten-free* cupcakes? Oh yeah!

All of us who are gluten-free have stories of how we got here, told through the events that led us down the path to the gluten-free lifestyle. If you're reading this paragraph, you probably have one, too, or know someone who does. Our story—the gluten-free part, at least—began in January 2007. It's a story that leads here, to this book of recipes for artisanal gluten-free cupcakes.

Like so many, our entry to the gluten-free world was medically motivated. After years of getting sicker, Pete was diagnosed with celiac disease. He became one of the estimated 1 in 133 Americans who has the autoimmune disorder. Almost overnight he'd joined a club he'd scarcely even heard of. There's no cure (though scientists are working on it), but there is a treatment: strict adherence to a gluten-free diet. For life.

It's no big deal, really, once you get the hang of it. But getting the hang of it is where the rubber meets the road. It can have a surprisingly steep learning curve and a surprisingly strong impact, not only on the foods we eat but also on our emotions and traditions—and, of course, on our health.

Within weeks of being gluten-free, Pete felt better than he had in years. Since then, life has only gotten better and better. We summited our first 20,000-foot mountain (technically, it was 19,974 feet, but who's counting?). Pete dabbled in *randonee* (ski mountaineering) and adventure racing. He competed in the U.S. national championship for Xterra off-road triathlons. And he took seventh place in a trail-running ultra-marathon that covered 51.4 miles and gained 10,000 vertical feet.

Contrary to what gluten eaters may think, going gluten-free wasn't the end. It was the beginning.

With our shared passion for food, Kelli's love of baking (plus some formal culinary training and a decade of restaurant and hospitality industry experience), and Pete's focus as a writer, we did what came naturally to us. We started developing recipes and writing about our gluten-free experiences on our blog, *No Gluten, No Problem.*

The blog title says it all when it comes to our gluten-free philosophy. No gluten? No problem! (Well, that and the "artisanal" thread that weaves its way through our food . . .)

Sure, there's a steep gluten-free learning curve in the beginning. Sure, you lose certain grains (namely, wheat, barley, rye, and cross-contaminated oats). And sure, you lose the *traditional* versions of foods made from those grains (bread, pasta, beer, cookies, cakes, etc.). But getting over the hump of that learning curve is like cresting a hill and beholding a beautiful panorama laid out before you.

It is an exciting time of potential and opportunity. It's a time of recovering health; of reinventing traditional family recipes and cultural foods; of comfort found in old, familiar ingredients (fruits and vegetables, nuts and seeds, whole meats and fish, and rice, corn, and potatoes); and of liberation found in a plethora of "new," unfamiliar ones (quinoa, millet, sorghum, buckwheat, and the list goes on . . .).

The experience brought us closer together, not just literally in the kitchen, but metaphorically as well in an emotional, relationship sense. When Pete went gluten-free, Kelli did, too. It was partly a pragmatic, strategic decision to minimize the potential for gluten cross-contamination in our kitchen. But it was also a decision born of the fact that we're both old-fashioned romantics, plain and simple. We wanted to toil and sweat in the kitchen together to produce one shared, common meal that we could then sit down and enjoy. And so we did. Many times.

These days, when it comes to gluten versus gluten-free foods, we want for nothing. We make (usually from scratch) and eat all the things we used to—breads, pizzas, lasagna, cookies, pancakes, waffles, you name it. In a sense, we had become our own living proof of the "no gluten, no problem" mantra. (In fact, many recipes coming out of the experience went into our first cookbook, *Artisanal Gluten-Free Cooking.*)

Along the way, two beautiful daughters came into our lives, and our gluten-free journey suddenly involved the joys (and the challenges) of parenthood. Our older daughter, Marin, proved highly sensitive to gluten. We suspect our younger daughter, Charlotte, is, too.

They are the deeper motivation (beyond our own sweet tooth) behind this book. Marin and Charlotte, in not too many years, will go to school. When they do, they'll almost certainly take part in elementary school parties, where cupcakes are often the treat of choice. (Sure, as of late cupcakes have been elevated to trendy status. But to an elementary school kid, cupcakes have always been cool.) We want our daughters to have the opportunity to take part in those childhood rites of passage, and so here we are, with the book you're holding in your hands.

But to come back to the opening questions: Why artisanal *gluten-free* cupcakes? Why gluten-free?

You might say, medically speaking, it's because we have to. You might say it was for our daughters. But you also might say, simply, that this is who we are, and when gluten-free cupcakes taste this good, why not?

our artisan gluten-free flour blend

A gluten-free cupcake, no matter how stellar the recipe, can only be as good as the flour blend on which it's built. The taste, texture, moisture, and crumb of the cake are all influenced by the flour (and indeed, depend upon it!). Every recipe is built upon the same solid foundation—our Artisan Gluten-Free Flour Blend. We spent months developing it, more months tweaking it, and years confirming that, in our opinion, it's one of the best all-purpose gluten-free flour blends you'll ever use for baking.

ARTISAN GLUTEN-FREE FLOUR BLEND

MAKES ABOUT 3 CUPS

1¼ cups (156 g) brown rice flour
¾ cup (88 g) sorghum flour
⅔ cup (84 g) cornstarch
¼ cup (148 g) potato starch
1 tablespoon plus 1 teaspoon (17 g) potato flour
1 teaspoon (3 g) xanthan gum

Combine all the ingredients, whisk thoroughly by hand to mix well, and store in an airtight container. (If you don't plan on using your flour soon or regularly, place the container in your refrigerator to preserve freshness.)

Note: Since the average cupcake recipe in this cookbook calls for 3 cups of flour per batch of 24 cupcakes, mixing up a single batch of the Artisan Gluten-Free Flour Blend is perfect for making one recipe. But if you're going to make more than one cupcake recipe or more than a single batch of cupcakes, then it will be worth it (and more convenient) to mix up a quadruple batch of flour, which yields about 12 cups:

5 cups (625 g) brown rice flour
3 cups (350 g) sorghum flour
2⅔ cups (360 g) cornstarch
1 cup (148 g) potato starch
¼ cup plus 4 teaspoons (57 g) potato flour
1 tablespoon plus 1 teaspoon (14 g) xanthan gum

FLOUR BLEND SUBSTITUTIONS

If you have a dietary sensitivity to a component of the Artisan Gluten-Free Flour Blend, not to worry! Try these ingredient substitutions to mix an alternative version of the flour blend that will match your dietary needs and still yield similar results in baking:

If you are sensitive to **sorghum,** omit the sorghum flour and use additional brown rice flour, so that a single batch will use **2 cups brown rice flour** total and a quadruple batch will use **8 cups brown rice flour** total.

If you are sensitive to **corn,** omit the cornstarch and use arrowroot flour instead. Use a shy ½ **cup arrowroot flour** for a single batch, and 1¾ **cups arrowroot flour** for a quadruple batch.

If you are sensitive to **potato,** omit the potato starch and potato flour and use tapioca starch instead. Use ⅓ **cup tapioca starch** for a single batch, and 1⅓ **cups tapioca starch** for a quadruple batch.

Note: For tapioca and arrowroot, "starch" and "flour" are interchangeable terms. Thus, for example, tapioca starch, tapioca flour, and tapioca starch flour are all the same thing and can be used interchangeably. However, this is not true for potato starch and potato flour, or for cornstarch and corn flour, which are distinct ingredients that cannot be substituted for each other.

ACCURATELY MEASURING FLOUR

All cups of flour aren't created equal. Depending on how you measure that cup, it may contain too much flour, too little flour, or just the right amount. It all comes down to density. On one end of the spectrum is sifted flour—light and airy. On the opposite end of the spectrum are packed cups of measured flour—dense and heavy. Compared to one cup of sifted Artisan Gluten-Free Flour Blend, one cup of packed Artisan Gluten-Free Flour Blend weighs *44 percent more*. That's a lot of extra flour.

For this cookbook, use the **spooned flour** method of measuring. Use a spoon to stir (and thus, lightly aerate) your master batch of flour. Then spoon the flour from your master batch into the measuring cup. Finally, level the measured cup of flour with a straight edge (such as a knife). If you prefer to bake **by weight,** 1 cup of Artisan Gluten-Free Flour Blend weighs **124 g**.

ingredients

For the most part, the ingredients used throughout this cookbook are straightforward. It helps to have some background information, though, about choosing the right type of each ingredient.

Gluten-free ingredients and prepared foods sit along a spectrum ranging from naturally gluten-free (e.g., apples) to may-or-may-not-be gluten-free (e.g., soy sauce) to traditionally *not* gluten-free (e.g., wheat pasta). In general, milk, cream, sugar, eggs, fruits, and nuts should all be naturally gluten-free. The component flours used to make the Artisan Gluten-Free Flour Blend (page 9) are specialty gluten-free ingredients. Other ingredients, such as extracts, sprinkles, and chocolate, *should* be gluten-free but might not be, depending on the company.

Throughout this cookbook we use the letters **GF** preceding certain ingredients to remind you to check the gluten-free status of a food that may or may not be gluten-free, depending on the source. It's a good policy to *always* review the ingredients label on any foods you buy, but pay special attention to ingredients denoted by a GF designation.

Baking Chocolate and Cocoa

Quality baking chocolate should be naturally gluten-free and made from only a handful of ingredients—unsweetened chocolate (cacao or cocoa solids), sugar, cocoa butter (cocoa fat), and sometimes milk fat or solids, vanilla, and an emulsifier. In this cookbook we call for only two types of chocolate: bittersweet and semi-sweet. Bittersweet chocolate has less sugar than semi-sweet and typically contains 60–85 percent cacao, resulting in a rich, intense (and more bitter) chocolate flavor. Semi-sweet chocolate has more sugar than bittersweet and typically contains 40–62 percent cacao. (In the United States, both types of chocolate must contain at least 35 percent total cacao.)

Baking chocolate is sold as bars, bricks, or squares or as chocolate baking chips.

Feel free to use either in our recipes, though we recommend baking chips (unless a recipe specifically calls for a bar of chocolate) because they are often significantly less expensive than an equal quantity of solid baking chocolate by weight. Ghirardelli, Nestlé, and Baker's are all widely available brands that make bittersweet and semisweet baking chocolate and are accepted to be gluten-free. (Each company's protocols differ, so check with each customer service department if you have any questions or concerns.)

Some of our recipes also call for cocoa powder. We use only natural unsweetened cocoa powder, which is naturally acidic and an important reactant with leavening agents such as baking soda. Cocoa powder is also sold in a second form—it's called Dutch-processed or alkalized. In this form the cocoa powder has been treated with an alkali to neutralize the chocolate's natural acidity. Do not use Dutch-processed or alkalized cocoa powder because it will not react with the baking soda in a recipe, thereby reducing the cake batter's rise during baking.

Butter

Unlike most cookbooks, our recipes call for *salted* butter. We prefer the flavor it imparts to the final cupcake—it brightens the flavor and makes a cupcake taste sweeter for a given amount of sugar. To balance the use of salted butter, our recipes typically call for about half as much salt as might normally be expected in a recipe. Those still concerned about their salt intake may use unsalted butter in our recipes as a straight substitution for the salted butter.

➡ Also see our guidelines on dairy-free baking (pages 246–252).

Candies and Sprinkles

A handful of recipes call for decorative sprinkles, and one—Chocolate Peanut Butter Cupcakes (page 123)—calls for Reese's mini peanut butter cup chocolate candies. Always check to ensure that the sprinkles and candy you're using are gluten-free.

Eggs

Our recipes call for Grade A large eggs. If you need to determine equivalencies for any reason (maybe you came home from the grocery store and realized that you—eek!—bought medium or extra-large eggs), a good rule of thumb is a large egg is about 3 tablespoons (1 tablespoon for the yolk and 2 tablespoons for the white). So, for example, if a cupcake recipe calls for 2 large eggs, use 6 tablespoons medium or extra-large eggs (2 large eggs x 3 tablespoons per egg = 6 tablespoons). For another example, if an Italian buttercream frosting calls for 4 large egg whites, use 8 tablespoons egg whites (4 large egg whites x 2 tablespoons per egg white = 8 tablespoons).

➡ Also see our guidelines on egg-free baking (pages 246–252).

Extracts and Oils

Many of our recipes call for extracts or oils, particularly vanilla, and less frequently, almond, maple, mint, or orange. Check to ensure that the version you're using is gluten-free. And *please,* use pure extracts and oils, not the artificial or imitation versions. As much as they try to mimic the real thing, their taste is too often fake. We're big fans of Rodelle's GF pure vanilla extract. McCormick's entire line of extracts is widely available and is gluten-free.

Flours

The only flours you'll need are the ones called for to mix up a batch of Artisan Gluten-Free Flour Blend. They are brown rice flour, sorghum flour, cornstarch, potato starch, and potato flour. We can't recommend highly enough the Bob's Red Mill brand of flours for this purpose. They're reliably gluten-free and of consistently high quality.

If you're averse to mixing up your own batch of our Artisan Gluten-Free Flour Blend, it is possible to use a store-bought all-purpose gluten-free flour blend. However, it's useful to keep a few words of wisdom in mind:

Although using a store-bought blend can be done with some degree of success, taste and texture will both suffer. Our recipes are developed using our Artisan Gluten-Free Flour Blend, and too often substituting another flour blend just doesn't measure up.

If you do opt to use a premade blend, try to stay away from ones that use bean flours (i.e., garbanzo/chickpea, fava), which result in undesirable textures and aftertaste.

Finally, because our Artisan Gluten-Free Flour Blend is built upon whole grain brown rice and sorghum flours as the primary ingredients, it contains more nutrients— and has a better protein-carbohydrate balance for baking—than many store-bought blends, which too often are based upon nutrient-poor cornstarch, potato starch, tapioca starch, and white rice flour for their main ingredients. (We also use cornstarch and potato starch in our blend but as minority ingredients to improve texture.)

The more closely a store-bought blend resembles the Artisan Gluten-Free Flour Blend, the better off you'll be in your cupcake baking.

➡ Though not a flour, it's important to note that our Artisan Gluten-Free Flour Blend includes a baseline level of xanthan gum, although our recipes also call for adding specific quantities of xanthan gum depending on the cupcake. If you opt to use a store-bought gluten-free flour blend and it does not include a baseline level of xanthan gum (or another gum, such as guar gum), you may need to add additional xanthan gum to the cupcake batter beyond what is called for in the recipe.

Food Coloring

One ingredient you *won't* find in this cookbook is food coloring, especially of the unnaturally bright artificial variety. Without digressing into a lengthy discussion, suffice it to say that we're not fans of pumping our cupcakes—and our bodies—full of artificial dyes. Every cupcake and frosting color you see in this book is 100 percent natural, made with homemade from-scratch fruit and vegetable purees and juices (with the rare exception of some colored sprinkles or a maraschino cherry here or there).

An increasing number of companies are selling natural food colorants derived primarily from fruits and vegetables. The Nature's Flavors and India Tree brands are two, and they're gluten-free (as always, double check to be sure!). If you use these natural food colorings, keep a few important things in mind: 1) If used in sufficient quantities, they can impart a flavor to your cupcakes. 2) Some may not hold up well to high-heat applications, such as baking. 3) Some may react with other ingredients in a recipe, such as natural red coloring made from beet juice, which often magically loses its color—see the headnote to our Red Velvet Cupcakes recipe (page 53) for more information. 4) They're expensive, on the order of $10 per ounce. But used in small quantities in icings and frostings—for example, when coloring a small batch of frosting orange to pipe tiny carrots on top of the frosting on your Carrot Cake Cupcakes (page 57)—these natural food colorings can be a good route.

Milks, Creams, and Cheeses

Typically, our cupcake recipes call for either milk and sour cream, or buttermilk. The sour cream and buttermilk replace all or a portion of additional milk that would otherwise be found in a gluten-based recipe. They give gluten-free cakes a more tender crumb.

We use 2 percent milk in our baking, though any milk will work in the recipes.

Buttermilk comes in three types—old fashioned (traditional), cultured, and acidified. We use cultured buttermilk in our baking, though again, any of the three will work in the recipes.

On the frosting side of the cupcake equation, we use a variety of creams and cheeses. Cream cheese is used for (surprise!) cream cheese frosting, ricotta and mascarpone cheeses are used for Italian-inspired cupcakes such as Tiramisu Cupcakes (page 237) and Cannoli Cupcakes (page 213), and half-and-half is used for Latin American–inspired cupcakes such as Dulce de Leche Cupcakes (page 223). (Our Italian buttercream contains only butter, as far as dairy goes.)

You'll find frosting recipes that call for heavy cream (also known as whipping cream or heavy whipping cream). We use it to make a variety of traditional and flavored whipped creams as well as our powdered sugar frostings (also known as American buttercream). It is typically sold in both pasteurized or ultra-pasteurized versions. If at all possible, use *pasteurized* heavy cream, *not* ultra-pasteurized heavy cream. Compared to pasteurized heavy cream, which reaches a maximum temperature of 161°F during the pasteurization process, ultra-pasteurized heavy cream reaches a maximum temperature of 275°F. The higher temperature gives ultra-pasteurized heavy cream a longer shelf life if left unopened in the refrigerator, but it breaks down the protein structure of the cream. In other words, it doesn't whip nearly as well as pasteurized heavy cream.

➡ Also see our guidelines on dairy-free baking (pages 246–252).

Sugars

Throughout this cookbook we use the term *sugar* to denote granulated cane sugar. The only other sugars called for are brown sugar and confectioners' sugar (also known as powdered sugar and used almost always in frostings).

➡ Also see our guidelines on refined-sugar-free baking (pages 246–252).

tools

The following is a fairly all-encompassing list of kitchen tools you'll use to bake our cupcakes and decorate them with frosting. Some are standard items you'll find in any kitchen, which will be used for every recipe. Others may come into service for a handful of recipes, and a few are inexpensive specialty items you might use only once or twice. By no means should you feel you need to own every one of these tools before you dive into making cupcakes. But we list them here so you can get a sense of our recommended tools of the cupcake trade. We use them regularly, and if you're as much a fan of baking cupcakes as we are, we have a pretty good feeling these tools will become some of your favorite go-to cupcake-making implements!

Bowls

Small, medium, and large sizes are indispensable for mixing. We mostly use the bowl from our KitchenAid stand mixer in combination with small and medium mixing bowls. They may be made of stainless steel or glass/Pyrex, but if you're also using your mixing bowls as part of a makeshift double boiler, as we do, at least some of them should be metal, which conducts heat better than glass does.

Candy Thermometer

Indispensable, period. It's a necessary tool to make caramel, Italian and Swiss buttercream, and other techniques (such as frying oil for the cannoli) turn out properly. A meat thermometer is insufficient because it doesn't read to high enough temperatures. Your candy thermometer should register up to 400°F.

Cheese Grater

A cheese grater is perfect for making larger shavings of chocolate (when shaved chocolate from a Microplane grater is too fine). We use it this way to finish off the Tiramisu Cupcakes (page 239).

Citrus Reamer

Usually made of wood or metal, a citrus reamer is a small, inexpensive, handheld tool for freshly juicing lemons, limes, and oranges.

Cookie Cutters

Some of our cupcakes, including S'mores Cupcakes (page 131) and Gingerbread Cupcakes (page 183), are topped with small, gluten-free cookies. The Maple Madness Cupcakes (page 243) use a maple leaf cutout traced from a cookie cutter, and the Cannoli Cupcakes (page 213) are topped with a from-scratch gluten-free cannolo made with a 2-inch round cookie cutter. Other than for these recipes, you won't need a cookie cutter.

Cookie Scoop

Although you can use a spoon to divide cupcake batter among the paper-lined cups of a cupcake tin, an appropriate-size cookie (or ice cream) scoop can be very convenient.

Cupcake Tins

Metal tins that hold 12 cupcakes each are the standard (compared to jumbo and mini cupcake tins). All our recipes yield 24 cupcakes—with the exception of Rum Raisin Cupcakes (page 197), which yields 18—so two cupcake tins will serve you well.

Double Boiler

A double boiler is used to evenly heat (and melt) certain foods such as chocolate without burning them. A lower chamber contains a small amount of boiling water. An upper chamber contains the food being heated. Since water (at sea level) boils at 212°F, the steam rising up and escaping past the upper chamber holds its temperature constant without risk of becoming too hot over the direct heat source (such as the gas flame of a stovetop burner). Although many companies sell dedicated double boilers, you can follow our lead by using a saucepan for your lower chamber and a metal mixing bowl nested on top for your upper chamber. (Be sure the water in the saucepan is not high enough to touch the bottom of the mixing bowl.)

Dowels

Wooden dowels—$\frac{1}{2}$ inch diameter by 4 inches long—are used to make from-scratch gluten-free cannoli to top the Cannoli Cupcakes. A long dowel rod can be purchased at most home improvement stores and cut to length. If you aren't making the Cannoli Cupcakes, you don't need the dowels.

Food Processor

A food processor is very useful for grinding nuts (pistachio, hazelnut, almond) as well as for making fruit purees (cherry, blueberry, strawberry, raspberry, pineapple). Some of the smaller quantities of fruit puree can also be done in a mini food processor, a common attachment for a handheld immersion blender.

Handheld Immersion Blender

A handheld immersion blender comes in handy for making certain sauces, such as our strawberry sauce. You can use a blender or even a food processor if you don't have a handheld immersion blender.

Knives

An all-purpose kitchen knife is useful for slicing fruit and chopping herbs. More often, though, we use a small paring knife. It is perfect for small detail cutting when preparing decorations (sliced strawberry and banana, finely diced mango), peeling and coring apples and pears, and coring and hollowing out cupcakes that are to be filled. (See also *Palette Knife.*)

Measuring Cups

There's not much to be said here. We use 'em. You will, too.

Measuring Spoons

See *Measuring Cups.*

Mesh Strainer

A fine mesh metal strainer is perfect for dusting cupcakes with cocoa powder or cinnamon.

Microplane Grater

Our favorite gadget for zesting lemons, limes, and oranges as well as for decorating cupcakes with finely shaved chocolate.

Mixers

Either a stand or handheld electric mixer is more or less a must-have for baking. Unless a recipe specifically calls for a stand mixer (as our Italian buttercream does), you can use either. When using a stand mixer, both the paddle and whisk attachments will come in handy. With a handheld electric mixer, the beaters stand in for both the paddle and whisk attachments of a stand mixer.

Palette Knife

Many bakers use an offset spatula to ice cupcakes. It's normally used to prevent your knuckles from contacting the frosting on a larger cake as you ice it. For cupcakes we think it's overkill, especially since you can hold individual cupcakes in your hand as you decorate them. For this task we much prefer a palette knife; its smaller size is better matched for decorating pint-size cakes.

Paper Cupcake Liners

With the exception of a handful of recipes when the cupcakes are baked directly in the tins, you'll line the cups of a cupcake tin with standard paper liners.

Pastry Bag

For cupcakes that call for piping on the frosting, reusable pastry bags are the way to go. They are like large cones fitted with piping tips on the end. You fill them with the frosting that you squeeze out through the piping tip and onto the cupcakes. If you don't have pastry bags, use scissors and nip off the *bottom* corner of a one-gallon zip-top bag, a cheap and easy alternative.

Pastry Brush

A pastry brush with either traditional hair or silicone bristles is ideal for "painting" the Tiramisu and Rum Raisin Cupcakes with their respective sauces. Otherwise, you won't need it.

Piping Tips: Circle, Star

Piping tips, often made of metal but sometimes of plastic, work in concert with pastry bags to enable you to make all sorts of elaborate decorations when frosting your cupcakes. They come in myriad shapes and sizes, but we find that just a few make possible an enormous variety of options. A mere two—a large open tip and a medium-large star tip—will enable you to make the majority of the frosting decoration styles in this book.

➡ For more specific information on particular piping tips and how to achieve different effects, see Decorating Tips (page 34).

Rolling Pin

From crushing nuts to rolling out cookie dough for the Gingerbread and Cannoli Cupcakes, a rolling pin comes in handy from time to time.

Saucepans

Saucepans serve a variety of functions, from making the sugar syrup for buttercreams, to preparing caramels, to melting butter, to making sauces, to serving as part of a makeshift double boiler. If possible, use heavy-bottom saucepans for candy making. They conduct and hold heat better and aren't as prone to developing hot spots.

Scale

A basic kitchen scale comes in very handy, especially for measuring chocolate.

Spatulas

Standard rubber spatulas are great for scraping down the sides and bottoms of mixing bowls and for making sure every last drop of batter gets into your cupcake liners.

Toothpicks

Wooden toothpicks inserted into the center of baked cupcakes are an easy way to double check that the cupcakes are done baking at the end of their allotted time.

Torch

A small butane kitchen torch is the way to go for toasting meringue and marshmallows, such as in our Lemon Meringue (page 195) and S'mores Cupcakes (page 131).

Vegetable Peeler

A vegetable peeler comes into use only once, for the Carrot Cake Cupcakes (page 57). It's used to peel the carrots that get shredded for the cupcakes and to make the candied carrot ribbons that top them off.

Whisk

A metal whisk is another standard you probably own already.

Wire Rack

A wire rack is perfect for cooling cupcakes and—when placed over a sheet tray—is a great way to let excess cocoa powder or cinnamon "fall through" when dusting cupcakes or for drizzled toppings (such as dulce de leche, caramel, or poured chocolate ganache) to ooze down the sides of the cupcakes without messing up plates, serving trays, or a cupcake tower.

Wooden Spoon

A wooden spoon, because it doesn't conduct heat the way a metal spoon does, is an excellent choice for making caramel and other high-temperature candies.

types of cakes

Throughout this cookbook you'll find an incredibly wide variety of cupcakes. They all pretty much fall into one of the following cake categories.

The High-Ratio Cake

Many cakes are traditionally based on four fundamental ingredients: flour, sugar, eggs, and fat (butter). The flour and eggs give the cake structure; the sugar and fat make it tender. A high-ratio cake is one that has more sugar than flour by weight. (Remember that it's the *weight* ratio that matters, not the volume. Since sugar weighs more than flour, a cake with 1 cup of sugar may have 1½ cups of flour and would still be a high-ratio cake.) Our standard high-ratio cake uses milk in combination with sour cream.

The Buttermilk Cake

Our buttermilk cake is simply a twist on our standard high-ratio cake. We use buttermilk in lieu of regular milk and sour cream, and whole eggs instead a blend of whole eggs and egg whites (as we do in our standard high-ratio cakes). Both our standard high-ratio cake and our buttermilk cake use baking powder, baking soda, or both for leavening.

The Sponge Cake

The Tiramisu and Hazelnutty Cupcakes (pages 239 and 106) are examples of sponge cakes, which use beaten eggs—either egg whites or whole eggs—for their leavening. For the Tiramisu Cupcakes, we boost the leavening with a little baking powder, but the taste and texture of the cupcake remain true to the sponge cake category.

The Flourless Cake

Unlike any other recipe in the book—and as their name implies—the Flourless Chocolate Cupcakes contain no flour, gluten-free or otherwise.

Flourless Chocolate Cupcake, *page 135*

The Doesn't-Have-a-Category Cake

The French Toast Cupcake (page 227) starts out more as a bread pudding and, as such, doesn't truly fit into any cake category.

types of frosting

In this cookbook you'll find six major types of frosting plus one that's notably absent. Here we explain what they are (and in the case of one, why we left it out).

American Buttercream

What we often call a powdered sugar frosting is more properly known as American buttercream. It is made by creaming together confectioners' sugar and fat. We use butter and heavy cream for the fat and finish it off with vanilla extract or other flavoring. The result is a very sweet frosting that packs a lot of punch.

Italian Buttercream

More complex to make than American buttercream, Italian buttercream is made by dissolving sugar in water and bringing the mixture to a temperature of 240°F. The heated sugar mixture is then drizzled into egg whites that have already been whipped into soft peaks. (The heat from the sugar

"cooks" the egg whites, so there's no food safety concern related to raw eggs.) Finally, fat (butter) and any flavoring are mixed in as well. The result is a rich, silky smooth frosting that's not overpoweringly sweet.

Swiss Buttercream

A single recipe—Poached Pearfection Cupcakes (page 235)—calls for Swiss buttercream. Egg whites and sugar are whisked together over a double boiler until they reach a temperature of 140°F (as with Italian buttercream, egg whites are rendered safe to eat by the heat). They are then added to a mixer and whisked at high speed until stiff peaks have formed and they have cooled to room temperature. Finally, the butter and flavoring are added, with a result similar to that of Italian buttercream.

Note: All buttercreams can be made in advance and stored in the refrigerator (for up to one week) or in the freezer

(for up to one month). To prepare for use in a recipe, set a chilled buttercream on the counter and let it come to room temperature. Then re-whisk briefly to make it smooth.

Cream Cheese Frosting

Our cream cheese frosting is like American buttercream in the sense that it's made with confectioners' sugar and butter (but no heavy cream). The major difference is the addition of cream cheese, which is creamed with the butter. Our cream cheese frosting is slightly less sweet than American buttercream. It makes a softer frosting that doesn't hold its shape as firmly as one made with more confectioners' sugar, but it also allows more of the cream cheese flavor to come through in the frosting.

Ganache

Ganache is a deliciously rich chocolate frosting that's deceptively simple to make. It comprises just two ingredients: bittersweet chocolate and cream. Heated cream is added to a mixing bowl that already contains chunks or chips of bittersweet chocolate. The heat from the cream melts the chocolate, and the mixture is stirred until it's uniform and smooth. Throughout this cookbook, we use three types of ganache:

1. Poured ganache uses more cream for a given quantity of chocolate. It remains more fluid, has a glossy finish, and, as its name implies, is poured over the cupcakes.
2. Spread ganache uses a little less cream than poured ganache so it sets up more at room temperature. It still has the glossy shine of poured ganache, but it can be spread on cupcakes with a small palette knife.
3. Whipped ganache starts as spread ganache, but when the spread ganache cools to room temperature, it is beaten with the paddle attachment of a stand mixer until it becomes lighter and fluffy with a matte finish.

Whipped Creams

Whipped creams are made with heavy whipping cream, confectioners' sugar, and flavoring (vanilla extract, mint oil, cinnamon, dulce de leche). They're delicious and simple, but it's easy to overwhip them.

Icings/Glazes

Made with confectioners' sugar and milk or lemon juice, glazes are relatively thin so they can be drizzled. They start out glossy when wet, but turn matte when dry.

We use them on our Crumb Cake Cupcakes (page 181) and Lemon Poppy Seed Cupcakes (page 83).

Rolled Fondant

Rolled fondant is popular on wedding cakes, and increasingly, it's showing up on cupcakes, too. It starts as smooth, satin sheets made with gelatin, glucose, glycerin, and confectioners' sugar. We *don't* use it. Why? We admit . . . when rolled fondant is done well, it can look great. But that's where the positives end. It's sorely lacking in the taste department, a major priority for us. Most people peel it off and leave it behind when they eat the cake beneath. That's not our style. We've made a very conscious effort to decorate every cupcake with fully edible ingredients you *want* to eat and that make sense for the cupcake's flavors. Also, rolled fondant can be difficult to work with, for novices especially but even for experienced bakers. Our emphasis is on accessible cupcakes with great taste and texture. By that measure, we'll take a buttercream over a fondant any day.

filled cupcakes

everal of our cupcakes are filled: the Boston Crème (page 163), Napoleon (page 171), and Fruit Tart Cupcakes (page 149) contain pastry cream; the Key Lime Pie Cupcakes (page 153) have a key lime filling; the Jelly Donut Cupcakes (page 157) have a strawberry filling; and the Caramel Apple Pie Cupcakes (page 165) have a cinnamon apple filling. Making filled cupcakes is easier than you might think.

2. Cut a circle, 1½ to 2 inches in diameter, such that you remove an inverted cone from the cupcake.

1. Insert a paring knife at roughly a 45-degree angle into the top of the cupcake, approximately ½ inch in from the edge of the cupcake.

3. Slice the tip off the cone and reserve the "cap" of the cupcake, which serves as a lid.

4. Taking care not to break through the bottom of the cupcake, use the knife to remove additional crumbs until you've cored the cupcake, leaving a hole with vertical sides.

5. Replace the cap on the cupcake. It is now ready to be filled as per the recipe.

Notes:

- It's best to complete the process for one cupcake before going on to the next. That way you'll be sure each cap fits the correct cupcake.
- When you slice the tips off the inverted cupcake cones and reserve the caps for the cupcakes, you'll be left with a pile of cupcake crumbs. Discard them, compost them, use them In a bread pudding, or nibble on them while you're completing your cupcakes. (We vote for the latter. . . .)

Boston Crème Cupcake, *page 163*

secrets of an italian buttercream

*O*f all the frostings in this book, Italian buttercream is the most complex. But don't let that scare you away! With these step-by-step photos as your guide, you'll be making delicious Italian buttercream in no time.

1. Mix the sugar and water in a heavy saucepan. Put a candy thermometer in the sugar mixture and heat to 240°F without stirring.

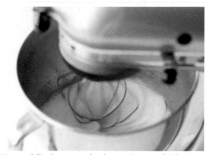

2. Meanwhile, in a stand mixer using a whisk attachment, whisk the egg whites and salt at medium-high speed until frothy.

3. Add the remaining 1 tablespoon of sugar to the egg whites and whisk until soft peaks form. Turn the mixer off and let the egg whites sit until the sugar comes up to temperature.

5. After all the sugar is added, continue whisking the mixture until it is cool, about 10 minutes.

4. When the sugar mixture reaches 240°F, with the mixer at medium speed slowly drizzle the hot sugar mixture down the side of the bowl into the beaten egg whites.

6. While the egg whites are whisking, cut the butter into tablespoon-size pieces.

7. When the egg whites are cool, leave the mixer running at medium speed and add the butter, 1 tablespoon at a time, allowing enough time for each tablespoon of butter to incorporate after each addition, until all the butter is added.

9. Switch to the paddle attachment, add any fruit purees, and mix for an additional 1 or 2 minutes at medium-high speed until the air bubbles are out of the frosting and the frosting is silky smooth.

8. Add the vanilla or any flavorings, and mix to combine.

getting friendly with your pastry bag and piping tips

*F*ollow these simple steps for prepping and filling a pastry bag with buttercream.

1. Fit a piping tip into a pastry bag. At the large open end of the bag, roll or invert the lip of the bag to create a "cuff."

2. Use a spatula to fill the open bag, trying to minimize any air bubbles or gaps in the frosting, which can cause problems when squeezed through the piping tip.

3. Unroll the open end of the bag, bring the bag together between the thumb and first finger, and twist the bag to cinch it down tight over the frosting.

4. Use the remaining fingers of that hand to provide even pressure on the pastry bag, forcing the frosting out through the piping tip. (Apply the pressure with your dominant hand and use your non-dominant hand to guide the piping tip.) As the pastry bag empties, re-twist the bag, cinch it closer to the piping tip, and continue frosting.

Note: If you don't have a pastry bag, snip off the corner of a large zip-top bag (one-gallon size). This technique works well as a stand-in for a piping bag fitted with an open tip. Simply cut the hole to your desired size. Keep in mind, however, that a zip-top bag is not as durable as a pastry bag and is not as easy to clean (for reuse) as a pastry bag. If you plan to make cupcakes with any regularity—and decorate them by piping on the frosting—a pastry bag and a handful of piping tips are a very worthwhile and inexpensive investment.

decorating tips

*F*ollow these basic instructions with accompanying photos for piping perfection—or pretty close to it!—when decorating your cupcakes.

open TIP SPIraL

Using an open tip (Ateco #808 or similar) and holding the pastry bag vertically or at a 45-degree angle, start at the outer edge of the cupcake and apply steady, even pressure to squeeze out the frosting. As you prepare to close the circle, without stopping, spiral the frosting to make a smaller circle atop the first. End the spiral in a swirl at the peak. (For a finished example, see Snickerdoodle Cupcakes, page 217.)

star TIP SPIraL

Use the directions for an open tip spiral (left) but use the Wilton #1M, Ateco #826, or similar. (For a finished example, see Orange Dreamsicle Cupcakes, page 201.)

DOLLOPS

Using an open tip (Wilton #12 or similar) and holding the pastry bag vertically, apply steady and even pressure to form a small dollop, then release the pressure, lifting the tip straight up. (For a finished example, see Mocha Cupcakes, page 143.)

FLORETTES

Also known as drop flowers. Using a star tip (Wilton #1M or similar), hold the pastry bag vertically with the tip close to the surface of the cupcake. Squeeze the bag, keeping the tip in place as frosting pushes out, forming the petals of the florette. Release pressure and pull away straight up. (For a finished example, see Lemon Blueberry Cupcakes, page 79.)

ROSETTES

Rosettes are basically twisted florettes using the star tip (Wilton #1M or similar). Follow the directions for the florette (bottom left), but as you apply pressure, twist the bag and tip to give the florette a mini swirl or spiral, creating the rosette. (For a finished example, see Orange Cranberry Cupcakes, page 87.)

PETALS

Using a petal tip (Wilton #124 or similar), hold the narrow end of the tip toward the center of the cupcake. As you apply pressure to the bag, rotate the tip in a C-shaped arc, keeping the narrow end of the tip near the center to form a petal. Repeat around the perimeter, then add additional smaller layers on top. (For a finished example, see Mango Mania Cupcakes, page 96.)

gluten-free baking tips

Temperature of Ingredients

Many of our recipes call for room temperature buttermilk, eggs, and butter. Room temperature ingredients yield a smoother, more uniform batter and are ideal for creaming together butter and sugar. If you don't have time to let those ingredients sit on the counter until they reach room temperature and they are still cold, that's okay, too. As you mix your cupcake batter, the batter might separate. Don't fret. It's not ruined, and the cupcakes will taste fine! Our recipes call for mixing at high speed for five seconds right at the end and immediately before transferring the batter to the cupcake tins, which will give you a smooth batter no matter the starting temperature of your ingredients.

Mixers

Throughout the cookbook we use the term *electric mixer* to denote either a stand mixer or a handheld electric mixer. Feel free to use either unless a recipe specifically calls for the use of a stand mixer.

Melting Chocolate

Several recipes in this cookbook call for melting chocolate or for melting and then cooling (to room temperature) chocolate. This can be done in one of two ways.

The shortcut method is to place the chocolate in a glass bowl and melt it in the microwave. Be very careful not to burn the chocolate. Microwave it just enough to soften it, then stir it with a rubber spatula to help it fully melt. If needed, you can always return it to the microwave for additional time to further soften.

The second method is to melt the chocolate in a double boiler (page 18), stirring just until it is completely melted.

Whisking Egg Whites

When whisking egg whites—for example, in meringue, buttercreams, and sponge cakes—our recipes call for either soft peaks or stiff peaks. For soft peaks, when the whisk is lifted out of the whipped egg whites, a "peak" will stand up and fall over. For stiff peaks, when the whisk is lifted out of the whipped egg whites, a "peak" will stand up and remain standing proud.

Mixing Versus Over-Mixing Cake Batter

Gluten-free cake batter can be sensitive to over-mixing, which will result in deflated cupcakes when baked. In the normal gluten-based creaming method of mixing, wet and dry ingredients are added alternately to the mixing bowl to ensure that everything is incorporated and well mixed. In a departure from that method, we add all the wet ingredients first followed by all the dry ingredients. Then we mix only as much as is called for in the recipe to avoid over-mixing.

Paper Versus Foil Liners

We strongly recommend using paper liners for your cupcake tins as opposed to foil liners. Paper liners "breathe," allowing excess moisture and steam to escape while the cupcakes bake. Foil liners, because they are impermeable, contain the steam, altering the texture of the finished cupcake. If you want the look of shiny silver or gold foil wrappers, you can always bake your cupcakes in plain liners and when

Chocolate Cupcakes with Vanilla Frosting, *page 43*

cooled slip a second, shiny foil wrapper over them for more dramatic visual effect.

Time Is of the Essence

After your batter is mixed, the clock starts ticking on the leavening. Immediately divide the batter among the paper-lined cups of your cupcake tins and put them in your preheated oven right away.

Dividing Batter

Our recipes call for evenly dividing the cupcake batter among the paper-lined cups of the cupcake tins. There are plenty of ways to do this, including using a spoon. However, an appropriate-size cookie or ice cream scoop can make this process easier and faster.

Smoothing the Raw Batter

Gluten-free cupcakes, as they bake, tend to hold the shape of their raw batter. The more you can smooth the tops of the raw cupcakes in the tins, the better the tops of your cupcakes will turn out. To smooth the tops of the cupcake batter, you can use a lightly oiled rubber spatula, or—our preference—two moistened fingers.

Choosing Cupcake Tins

We strongly recommend using light metal tins for baking. Dark metal attracts more heat and cooks cupcakes faster, resulting in more browning. Our recipes assume that a standard cupcake tin holds 12 cupcakes and that you will bake a batch of 24 cupcakes with two tins in your oven at the same time.

High-Altitude Baking

Add ¼ cup additional Artisan Gluten-Free Flour Blend to a full batch of cupcakes.

Metric Conversions

➡ If you use metric measurements or prefer to bake by weight, please consult the Metric Conversion Charts on page 253.

PART TWO

GET
BAKING!

classics

These time-tested cupcakes feature traditional flavors such as vanilla, chocolate, and red velvet. They're simple and straightforward, and they deliver every time. When you're looking for all-American cupcakes, look no further than these core classics.

Chocolate Cupcake with Vanilla Frosting

chocolate cupcakes
with vanilla frosting

Classic and kid friendly, this cupcake is a sure thing. The rich chocolate cake and fluffy Vanilla Frosting were a hit at our daughter Marin's first birthday party.

1 cup salted butter (2 sticks)

1 cup water

½ cup unsweetened cocoa powder (regular or dark)

2 cups sugar

2 large eggs

1 cup sour cream

1 teaspoon GF pure vanilla extract

2½ cups Artisan Gluten-Free Flour Blend (page 10)

2 teaspoons xanthan gum

1½ teaspoons GF baking powder

1½ teaspoons GF baking soda

½ teaspoon salt

Vanilla Frosting (recipe follows)

GF chocolate sprinkles

TO MAKE THE CUPCAKES:

1. Preheat the oven to 350°F. Line standard cupcake tins with paper liners.

2. Heat the butter, water, and cocoa over medium heat in a saucepan until the butter is melted.

3. Meanwhile, put the sugar in a mixing bowl. Add the butter-cocoa mixture and mix at low speed for about 5 minutes, until the mixture is cool.

4. Add the eggs one at a time, mixing to incorporate after each addition.

5. Add the sour cream and vanilla, mix to incorporate, and scrape down the sides of the bowl.

6. In a separate bowl, combine the flour, xanthan gum, baking powder, baking soda, and salt, and mix with a whisk to "sift" the ingredients and break up any lumps.

7. Add the dry ingredients to the cocoa-sour cream mixture and mix for about 10 seconds at medium-low speed to incorporate.

8. Scrape down the sides of the bowl and mix for an additional 5 seconds at high speed, just until everything is mixed and smooth.

9. Divide the batter evenly among the paper-lined cups. Make the top of the batter as smooth as you can.

10. Bake for 25 minutes.

11. Allow the cupcakes to cool in the tins for 10 minutes, then remove from the tins and let cool completely on a wire rack.

12. While the cupcakes are cooling, make the Vanilla Frosting.

TO FINISH THE CUPCAKES:

13. Use a small palette knife to spread the Vanilla Frosting on the cupcakes.

14. Garnish with chocolate sprinkles.

Note: To make Chocolate Cupcakes with Chocolate Frosting (another classic flavor combo!), combine the chocolate cake in this recipe with the chocolate frosting used in Vanilla Cupcakes with Chocolate Frosting (page 45).

VANILLA FROSTING

1 cup salted butter, room temperature
4 cups confectioners' sugar
¼ cup heavy cream
1 teaspoon GF pure vanilla extract

Cream together the butter, confectioners' sugar, cream, and vanilla until light and fluffy. If the frosting is too thick, add additional heavy cream, 1 teaspoon at a time, until you have the desired consistency.

vanilla cupcakes
with chocolate frosting

This cupcake with fudgy chocolate frosting is a classic combo loved by many. If there was such an thing as a Holy Trinity of Cupcakes, this would be one of the three (alongside its reciprocal, Chocolate Cupcakes with Vanilla Frosting, as well as Red Velvet Cupcakes). It's a straightforward and simple recipe that's easy to make and kid friendly.

¾ cup salted butter (1½ sticks), room temperature

1¾ cups sugar

2 teaspoons GF pure vanilla extract

2 large eggs, room temperature

2 large egg whites, room temperature

1 cup milk

¼ cup sour cream

3 cups Artisan Gluten-Free Flour Blend (page 10)

2 teaspoons xanthan gum

2½ teaspoons GF baking powder

1 teaspoon GF baking soda

½ teaspoon salt

Chocolate Frosting (recipe follows)

TO MAKE THE CUPCAKES:

1. Preheat the oven to 350°F. Line standard cupcake tins with paper liners.

2. With an electric mixer, cream together the butter and sugar until fluffy, then add the vanilla.

3. Add the eggs and egg whites one at a time, mixing to incorporate after each addition.

4. Add the milk and sour cream, and mix until combined.

5. In a separate bowl, combine the flour, xanthan gum, baking powder, baking soda, and salt, and mix with a whisk to "sift" the ingredients and break up any lumps.

6. Add the dry ingredients all at once to the sugar mixture and mix for about 10 seconds at medium-low speed to incorporate.

7. Scrape down the sides of the bowl and mix at high speed for about 5 seconds, just until the batter is completely mixed and smooth.

8. Divide the batter evenly among the paper-lined cups. Make the top of the batter as smooth as you can.
9. Bake for 25 minutes.
10. Allow the cupcakes to cool in the tins for 10 minutes, then remove from the tins and let cool completely on a wire rack.

11. While the cupcakes are cooling, make the Chocolate Frosting.

TO FINISH THE CUPCAKES:

12. Use a small palette knife to spread a swirl of Chocolate Frosting on the cupcakes.

CHOCOLATE FROSTING

1 cup salted butter (2 sticks)
4 cups confectioners' sugar
½ cup unsweetened cocoa powder
¼ cup plus 2 tablespoons heavy cream
2 teaspoons GF pure vanilla extract
½ cup GF semi-sweet chocolate chips or pieces, melted

1. Cream together the butter, confectioners' sugar, cocoa powder, cream, and vanilla until light and fluffy.
2. Mix in the melted chocolate. If the frosting is too thick, add additional heavy cream, 1 teaspoon at a time, until you have the desired consistency.

Vanilla Cupcake with Chocolate Frosting

White on White Cupcakes

white on white cupcakes

Vanilla lovers rejoice! This is a vanilla cupcake topped with Vanilla Buttercream. Add some multicolored sprinkles for a dash of color, or keep it clean and simple with nothing but the white on white.

¾ cup salted butter (1½ sticks), room temperature

1¾ cups sugar

2 teaspoons GF pure vanilla extract

2 large eggs, room temperature

2 large egg whites, room temperature

1 cup milk

¼ cup sour cream

3 cups Artisan Gluten-Free Flour Blend (page 10)

2 teaspoons xanthan gum

2½ teaspoons GF baking powder

1 teaspoon GF baking soda

½ teaspoon salt

Vanilla Buttercream (recipe follows)
GF multicolored sprinkles

TO MAKE THE CUPCAKES:

1. Preheat the oven to 350°F. Line standard cupcake tins with paper liners.

2. With an electric mixer, cream together the butter and sugar until fluffy, then add the vanilla.

3. Add the eggs and egg whites one at a time, mixing to incorporate after each addition.

4. Add the milk and sour cream, and mix until combined.

5. In a separate bowl, combine the flour, xanthan gum, baking powder, baking soda, and salt, and mix with a whisk to "sift" the ingredients and break up any lumps.

6. Add the dry ingredients all at once to the sugar mixture and mix for about 10 seconds at medium-low speed to incorporate.

7. Scrape down the sides of the bowl and mix at high speed for about 5 seconds, just until the batter is completely mixed and smooth.

8. Divide the batter evenly among the paper-lined cups. Make the top of the batter as smooth as you can.

9. Bake for 25 minutes.

10. Allow the cupcakes to cool in the tins for 10 minutes, then remove from the tins and let cool completely on a wire rack.

11. While the cupcakes are cooling, make the Vanilla Buttercream.

TO FINISH THE CUPCAKES:

12. Use a small palette knife to spread the Vanilla Buttercream on the cupcakes.

13. Garnish with the sprinkles.

VANILLA BUTTERCREAM

1⅓ cups plus 1 tablespoon sugar, divided

½ cup water

4 large egg whites

¼ teaspoon salt

**1½ cups salted butter (3 sticks), removed from the refrigerator
when you start the buttercream**

2 teaspoons GF pure vanilla extract

1. Mix 1⅓ cups of the sugar and the water in a heavy saucepan. Put a candy thermometer in the sugar mixture and heat to 240°F without stirring.
2. Meanwhile, in a stand mixer using the whisk attachment, whisk the egg whites and salt at medium-high speed until frothy.
3. Add the remaining 1 tablespoon of sugar to the egg whites and whisk until soft peaks form. Turn the mixer off and let the egg whites sit until the sugar mixture comes up to temperature.
4. When the sugar mixture reaches 240°F, with the mixer at medium speed slowly drizzle the sugar mixture down the side of the bowl into the beaten egg whites.
5. After all the sugar is added, continue whisking the mixture until it is cool, about 10 minutes.
6. While the egg whites are whisking, cut the butter into tablespoon-size pieces.
7. When the egg whites are cool, leave the mixer running at medium speed and add the butter, 1 tablespoon at a time, allowing enough time for each tablespoon of butter to incorporate after each addition, until all the butter is added.
8. Add the vanilla and mix to combine.
9. Switch to the paddle attachment and mix for an additional 1 to 2 minutes at medium-high speed until the air bubbles are out of the frosting and the frosting is silky smooth.

Red Velvet Cupcake

red velvet cupcakes

There are many stories about the origins of red velvet cake, both the cake itself and how it got its name. The earliest red velvet cakes were leavened with whipped egg whites. The modern-day red velvet cake, however, is leavened with buttermilk, vinegar, and baking soda. Either way, it's a cake with a light chocolaty flavor, dyed red, and finished with a white frosting—sometimes buttercream, but more often cream cheese. The contemporary baking soda red velvet cake presents a unique problem for bakers like us, who prefer natural dye over ounces of artificial red dye. The obvious choice is to use beet juice, which turns the batter a beautiful, deep magenta color, but the beet juice reacts with the baking soda during baking and turns brown. People these days expect a buttermilk red velvet, however, so that's what we give 'em. And we do use beet juice, which gives the cake a magenta "shell," but the core of the cupcake will mostly turn brown. This is not a mistake you (or we) make. Most important, the taste is unaffected. Close your eyes, and this red velvet will taste as good as any you've had.

½ cup salted butter (1 stick), room temperature

1½ cups sugar

1 teaspoon GF pure vanilla extract

2 large eggs, room temperature

1 cup buttermilk, room temperature

½ cup beet juice, freshly made with a juicer (see Note, next page)

1 tablespoon lemon juice

2¾ cups Artisan Gluten-Free Flour Blend (page 10)

1½ teaspoons xanthan gum

3 tablespoons unsweetened cocoa powder

½ teaspoon salt

1 tablespoon white vinegar

1½ teaspoons GF baking soda

Cream Cheese Frosting (recipe follows)

TO MAKE THE CUPCAKES:

1. Preheat the oven to 350°F. Line standard cupcake tins with paper liners.

2. With an electric mixer, cream together the butter and sugar until light and fluffy, then add the vanilla.

3. Add the eggs one at a time, mixing to

incorporate after each addition.

4. Add the buttermilk, beet juice, and lemon juice, and mix until combined.

5. In a separate bowl, combine the flour, xanthan gum, cocoa powder, and salt, and mix with a whisk to "sift" the ingredients and break up any lumps.

6. Add the dry ingredients all at once to the sugar mixture and mix for about 10 seconds at medium-low speed to incorporate. Scrape down the sides of the bowl.

7. In a separate small bowl, mix the vinegar and baking soda. Immediately add the vinegar mixture to the prepared batter and mix at high speed for about 5 seconds, just until the batter is completely mixed and smooth.

8. Divide the batter evenly among the paper-lined cups. Make the top of the batter as smooth as you can.

9. Bake for 25 minutes.

10. Allow the cupcakes to cool in the tins for 10 minutes, then remove from the tins and let cool completely on a wire rack.

11. While the cupcakes are cooling, make the Cream Cheese Frosting.

TO FINISH THE CUPCAKES:

12. Use a small palette knife to spread the frosting on the cupcakes.

Note: If you don't have a juicer, you can make beet juice by grating washed, peeled beets. Add the grated beets to a blender with a little bit of water and blend to make a beet puree. Then strain with cheese cloth or a fine mesh strainer.

CREAM CHEESE FROSTING

12 ounces cream cheese, room temperature
1 cup salted butter (2 sticks), room temperature
3¾ cups confectioners' sugar
1½ teaspoons GF pure vanilla extract

1. With an electric mixer, cream together the cream cheese and butter until completely incorporated.
2. Add the confectioners' sugar and vanilla, and mix until smooth and of spreading consistency. (Additional confectioners' sugar can be added to make a thicker frosting if needed.)

Carrot Cake Cupcakes

carrot cake cupcakes

MAKES 24 CUPCAKES

This cupcake is basically a classic carrot cake with cream cheese frosting shrunk to the pint-size portion of individual cupcakes. Thanks to the carrot, pineapple, and coconut, it's a very moist cake. In a unique twist, we garnish it with a quasi-candied ribbon of carrot.

2 cups sugar

1 cup vegetable oil

1 teaspoon GF pure vanilla extract

4 large eggs

2 cups shredded carrot (about 4 medium carrots)

1 cup flaked, sweetened coconut

²⁄₃ cup crushed pineapple (about one 8-ounce can)

2¾ cups Artisan Gluten-Free Flour Blend (page 10)

1½ teaspoons xanthan gum

1½ teaspoons GF baking powder

1½ teaspoons GF baking soda

2 teaspoons ground cinnamon

Cream Cheese Frosting (recipe follows)

Candied Carrot Ribbons (recipe follows)

TO MAKE THE CUPCAKES:

1. Preheat the oven to 350°F. Line standard cupcake tins with paper liners.

2. With an electric mixer, mix together the sugar and oil, then add the vanilla.

3. Add the eggs one at a time, mixing to incorporate after each addition.

4. Add the carrot, coconut, and pineapple, and mix until combined.

5. In a separate bowl, combine the flour, xanthan gum, baking powder, baking soda, and cinnamon, and mix with a whisk to "sift" the ingredients and break up any lumps.

6. Add the dry ingredients all at once to the sugar mixture and mix for about 10 seconds at medium-low speed to incorporate.

7. Scrape down the sides of the bowl and mix at high speed for about 5 seconds, just until the batter is completely mixed and smooth.

8. Divide the batter evenly among the paper-lined cups. Make the top of the batter as smooth as you can.
9. Bake for 30 minutes.
10. Allow the cupcakes to cool in the tins for 10 minutes, then remove from the tins and let cool completely on a wire rack.
11. While the cupcakes are cooling, make the Cream Cheese Frosting and the Candied Carrot Ribbons.

TO FINISH THE CUPCAKES:
12. Use a small palette knife to spread the Cream Cheese Frosting on top of the cupcakes.
13. Garnish with a Candied Carrot Ribbon.

CREAM CHEESE FROSTING

12 ounces cream cheese, room temperature
1 cup salted butter (2 sticks), room temperature
3¾ cups confectioners' sugar
1½ teaspoons GF pure vanilla extract

1. With an electric mixer, cream together the cream cheese and butter until completely incorporated.
2. Add the confectioners' sugar and vanilla, and mix until smooth and of spreading consistency. (Use additional confectioners' sugar to make a thicker frosting if needed.)

CANDIED CARROT RIBBONS

2 carrots
1 cup sugar
1 cup water

1. Peel the carrots. Then, to make the carrot ribbons, run the peeler the full length of each carrot in single, long strokes.
2. In a small saucepan, mix the sugar and water and heat over high heat to bring to a boil.
3. Add the carrot ribbons and cook for about 3 to 5 minutes, until the carrots are tender. Turn off the heat and remove the carrots.
4. Lay the carrots flat on a plate to let them cool. The remaining syrup can be used as a lightly carrot-infused simple syrup (perhaps in cocktails or sorbets) or can be discarded.

fruity

With bright, fresh flavors, these fruity cupcakes use citrus, berries, and other fruits to create colorful, moist cupcakes. The recipes are best paired with the seasons during which the various fruits are at their peak, though you can often substitute frozen fruit to make a year-round treat.

Strawberry Shortcake Cupcake

strawberry shortcake cupcakes

MAKES 24 CUPCAKES

Strawberry shortcake is a classic layered shortcake with whipped cream and strawberries between each cake layer and on top of the cake. The strawberries are often first dusted with sugar and allowed to sit, which makes them both sweeter and juicier. We prefer, however, to use fresh sliced strawberries sans sugar for a cleaner flavor (and a less messy cupcake!).

¾ cup salted butter (1½ sticks), room
    temperature

1¾ cups sugar

2 teaspoons GF pure vanilla extract

2 large eggs, room temperature

2 large egg whites, room temperature

1 cup milk

¼ cup sour cream

3 cups Artisan Gluten-Free Flour
    Blend (page 10)

2 teaspoons xanthan gum

2½ teaspoons GF baking powder

1 teaspoon GF baking soda

½ teaspoon salt

Whipped Cream (recipe follows)

1 quart strawberries, hulled and
    sliced

TO MAKE THE CUPCAKES:

1. Preheat the oven to 350°F. Line standard cupcake tins with paper liners.

2. With an electric mixer, cream together the butter and sugar until fluffy, then add the vanilla.

3. Add the eggs and egg whites one at a time, mixing to incorporate after each addition.

4. Add the milk and sour cream, and mix until combined.

5. In a separate bowl, combine the flour, xanthan gum, baking powder, baking soda, and salt, and mix with a whisk to "sift" the ingredients and break up any lumps.

6. Add the dry ingredients all at once to the sugar mixture and mix for about 10 seconds at medium-low speed to incorporate.

7. Scrape down the sides of the bowl and mix at high speed for about 5 seconds, just until the batter is completely mixed and smooth.

8. Divide the batter evenly among the paper-lined cups. Make the top of the batter as smooth as you can.

9. Bake for 25 minutes.

10. Allow the cupcakes to cool in the tins for 10 minutes, then remove from the tins and let cool completely on a wire rack.

11. While the cupcakes are cooling, hull and slice the strawberries and make the Whipped Cream.

TO FINISH THE CUPCAKES:

12. Remove the paper liners. With a serrated knife, slice each cupcake in half horizontally.

13. Spread a small amount of Whipped Cream on the cut side of the bottom half, and layer on a few strawberry slices.

14. Spread a small amount of Whipped Cream on the cut side of the top half and place onto the strawberry slices of the bottom half.

15. Spread additional Whipped Cream on top of the cupcake and garnish with strawberry slices.

WHIPPED CREAM

2 cups heavy cream
2 tablespoons confectioners' sugar
2 teaspoons GF pure vanilla extract

1. Chill a metal mixing bowl and a whisk or eggbeaters in the freezer for 5 minutes.

2. Pour the cream into the cold bowl and whisk until it starts to thicken.

3. Add the confectioners' sugar and vanilla, and whisk until soft peaks form. Do not over-mix or the over-whipped cream will take on a curdled appearance. (If this does happen, it's purely a cosmetic issue and won't affect the taste of your whipped cream.)

apple upside-down cupcakes

MAKES 24 CUPCAKES

Like a classic upside-down cake, these cupcakes reveal their true nature when flipped onto their heads, exposing the sliced apples beneath. It's a simple cupcake—no frosting, not overly sweet—but the combination of caramelized sugar and sweet apples sets it apart.

Caramel Sauce (recipe follows)

Melted butter or nonstick cooking spray

1 to 3 apples, thinly sliced (see Note, next page)

¾ cup salted butter (1½ sticks), room temperature

1¾ cups sugar

2 teaspoons GF pure vanilla extract

2 large eggs, room temperature

2 large egg whites, room temperature

1 cup milk

¼ cup sour cream

3 cups Artisan Gluten-Free Flour Blend (page 10)

2 teaspoons xanthan gum

2½ teaspoons GF baking powder

1 teaspoon GF baking soda

½ teaspoon salt

1. First, make the Caramel Sauce.

TO MAKE THE CUPCAKES:

2. Preheat the oven to 350°F. Brush standard cupcake tins with the melted butter.

3. Divide the Caramel Sauce among the cups of the tins and arrange the apple slices in the bottom of each cup.

4. With an electric mixer, cream together the butter and sugar until fluffy, then add the vanilla.

5. Add the eggs and egg whites one at a time, mixing to incorporate after each addition.

6. Add the milk and sour cream, and mix until combined.

7. In a separate bowl, combine the flour, xanthan gum, baking powder, baking soda, and salt, and mix with a whisk to "sift" the ingredients and break up any lumps.

8. Add the dry ingredients all at once to the sugar mixture and mix for about 10 seconds at medium-low speed to incorporate.

9. Scrape down the sides of the bowl and mix at high speed for about 5 seconds,

just until the batter is completely mixed and smooth.

10. Divide the batter evenly among the prepared cups. Make the top of the batter as smooth as you can.
11. Bake for 25 minutes.
12. Allow the cupcakes to cool in the tins for 5 minutes.
13. Remove from the tins by flipping the tins over onto a large platter.

TO FINISH THE CUPCAKES:

14. Serve the cupcakes warm or at room temperature.

Note: When slicing the apples, you can either cut traditional wedge-shaped thin slices or peel the apple, cut it into cross-sections, remove the core from each slice, and trim the outer edge of each "disc" of apple to make it fit in the bottom of the cupcake tins.

CARAMEL SAUCE

6 tablespoons salted butter (¾ stick)
¾ cup packed brown sugar
3 tablespoons water

1. Melt the butter in a sauté pan.
2. Stir in the brown sugar and water and simmer for 1 minute, stirring constantly.

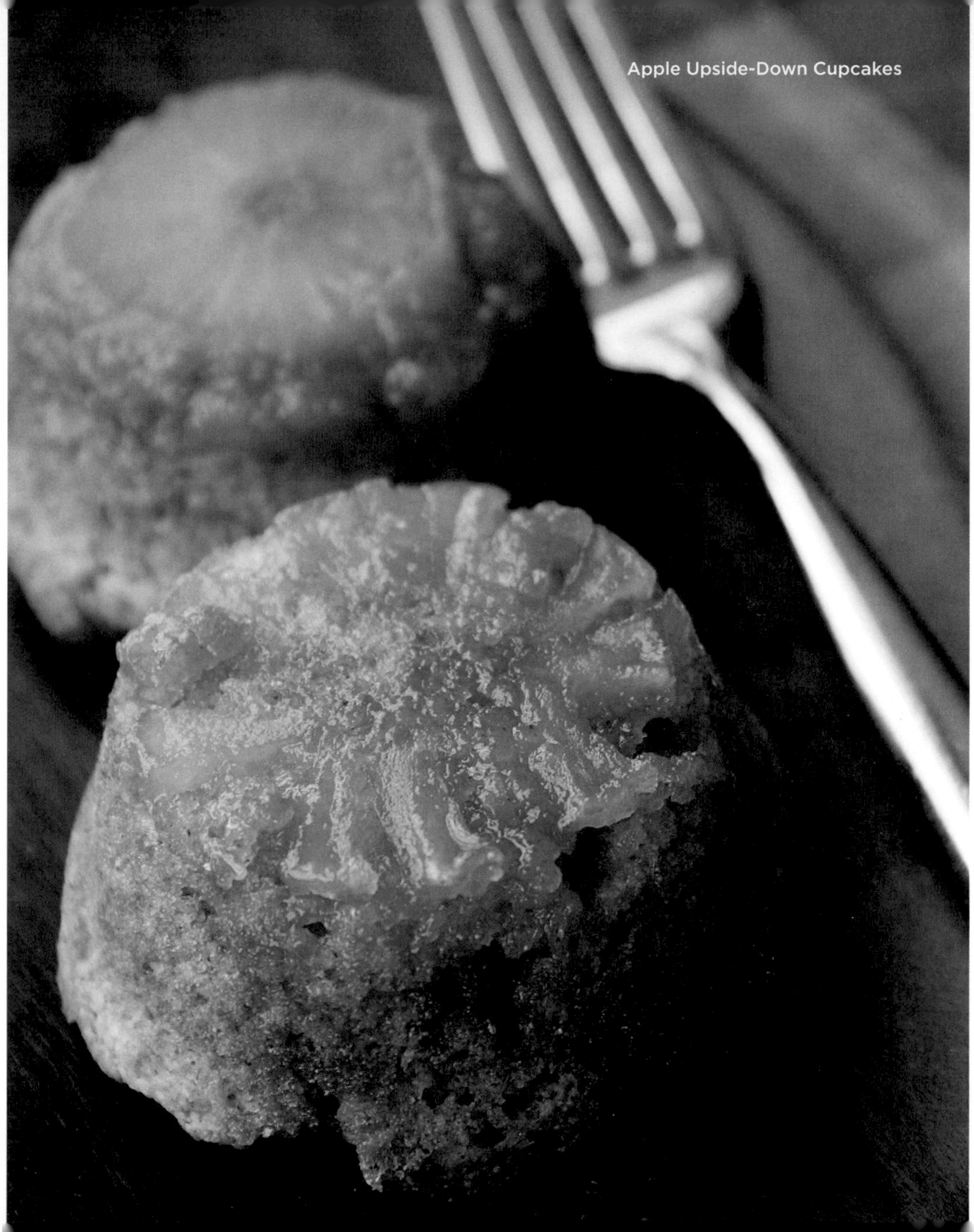
Apple Upside-Down Cupcakes

Bananas Foster Cupcakes

bananas foster cupcakes

A dish born in New Orleans, bananas Foster features cooked bananas in a sauce made with butter, brown sugar, and rum (and is often prepared by flambéing tableside in restaurants). It can be served solo, with vanilla ice cream, over crepes, and in myriad other ways. Here, we make a proper bananas Foster and then incorporate it into cupcakes in two distinct ways. We split the bananas Foster, taking the bananas themselves and folding them into the cupcake batter and taking the caramelized sauce and folding it into the buttercream. The result is a rich, banana-infused cupcake that says bananas Foster from head to toe.

¾ cup salted butter (1½ sticks), room temperature

1¾ cups sugar

2 teaspoons GF pure vanilla extract

2 large eggs, room temperature

2 large egg whites, room temperature

1 cup milk

¼ cup sour cream

3 cups Artisan Gluten-Free Flour Blend (page 10)

2 teaspoons xanthan gum

2½ teaspoons GF baking powder

1 teaspoon GF baking soda

½ teaspoon salt

Bananas Foster (recipe follows)

Bananas Foster Buttercream (recipe follows)

1. First, make the Bananas Foster.

TO MAKE THE CUPCAKES:

2. Preheat the oven to 350°F. Line standard cupcake tins with paper liners.

3. With an electric mixer, cream together the butter and sugar until fluffy, then add the vanilla.

4. Add the eggs and egg whites one at a time, mixing to incorporate after each addition.

5. Add the milk and sour cream, and mix until combined.

6. In a separate bowl, combine the flour, xanthan gum, baking powder, baking soda, and salt, and mix with a whisk to "sift" the ingredients and break up any lumps.

7. Add the dry ingredients all at once to the sugar mixture and mix for about

10 seconds at medium-low speed to incorporate.

8. Scrape down the sides of the bowl and mix at high speed for about 5 seconds, just until the batter is completely mixed and smooth.

9. Use a large rubber spatula to fold in the reserved bananas from the Bananas Foster.

10. Divide the batter evenly among the paper-lined cups. Make the top of the batter as smooth as you can.

11. Bake for 25 minutes.

12. Allow the cupcakes to cool in the tins for 10 minutes, then remove from the tins and let cool completely on a wire rack.

13. While the cupcakes are cooling, make the Bananas Foster Buttercream.

TO FINISH THE CUPCAKES:

14. Use a large open tip to pipe a spiral of Bananas Foster Buttercream on the cupcakes.

15. Serve with additional Bananas Foster, if desired.

BANANAS FOSTER

The Bananas Foster Cupcake recipe calls for a single batch of this. However, if desired, make a double batch and reserve half to decorate and serve with the cupcakes.

4 bananas
½ cup salted butter (1 stick)
½ cup packed brown sugar
¼ cup orange juice
¼ cup dark rum

1. Peel the bananas, quarter them lengthwise, and slice into ¼-inch thick pieces. Set aside.
2. Melt the butter in a sauté pan over medium heat.
3. Add the brown sugar and stir, cooking until the sugar is dissolved.
4. Add the bananas to the sugar mixture and cook for about 3 minutes, or until the bananas are soft.
5. Add the orange juice and rum, and simmer for 1 minute. Remove the pan from the heat.
6. Using a slotted spoon or a fork, remove all the banana pieces and set aside. Reserve the sauce.

BANANAS FOSTER BUTTERCREAM

1⅓ cups plus 1 tablespoon sugar, divided

½ cup water

4 large egg whites

¼ teaspoon salt

**1½ cups salted butter (3 sticks), removed from the refrigerator
when you start the buttercream**

Reserved sauce from the Bananas Foster (recipe on previous page)

1. Mix 1⅓ cups of the sugar and the water in a heavy saucepan. Put a candy thermometer in the sugar mixture and heat to 240°F without stirring.
2. Meanwhile, in a stand mixer using a whisk attachment, whisk the egg whites and salt at medium-high speed until frothy.
3. Add the remaining 1 tablespoon of sugar to the egg whites and whisk until soft peaks form. Turn the mixer off and let the egg whites sit until the sugar comes up to temperature.
4. When the sugar mixture reaches 240°F, with the mixer at medium speed, slowly drizzle the hot sugar mixture down the side of the bowl into the beaten egg whites.
5. After all the sugar is added, continue whisking the mixture until it is cool, about 10 minutes.
6. While the egg whites are whisking, cut the butter into tablespoon-size pieces.
7. When the egg whites are cool, leave the mixer running at medium speed and add the butter, 1 tablespoon at a time, allowing enough time for each tablespoon of butter to incorporate after each addition, until all the butter is added.
8. Switch to the paddle attachment and add the reserved sauce from the Bananas Foster. Mix for an additional 1 or 2 minutes at medium-high speed until the air bubbles are out of the frosting and the frosting is silky smooth.

cherry vanilla cupcakes

The words cherry vanilla *make us think of an old-fashioned soda flavor, but they also happen to make for a great cupcake flavor, too. This version is a vanilla cupcake with diced cherries folded into the cake, topped with a cherry-flecked Cherry Vanilla Buttercream.*

¾ cup salted butter (1½ sticks),
  room temperature

1¾ cups sugar

1 teaspoon GF pure almond extract

2 large eggs, room temperature

2 large egg whites, room temperature

1 cup milk

¼ cup sour cream

3 cups Artisan Gluten-Free Flour
  Blend (page 10)

2 teaspoons xanthan gum

2½ teaspoons GF baking powder

1 teaspoon GF baking soda

½ teaspoon salt

2 cups pitted whole cherries (frozen or
  fresh), diced (see Note, next page)

Cherry Vanilla Buttercream (recipe
  follows)

TO MAKE THE CUPCAKES:

1. Preheat the oven to 350°F. Line standard cupcake tins with paper liners.

2. With an electric mixer, cream together the butter and sugar until fluffy, then add the vanilla.

3. Add the eggs and egg whites one at a time, mixing to incorporate after each addition.

4. Add the milk and sour cream and mix until combined.

5. In a separate bowl, combine the flour, xanthan gum, baking powder, baking soda, and salt, and mix with a whisk to "sift" the ingredients and break up any lumps.

6. Add the dry ingredients all at once to the sugar mixture and mix for about 10 seconds at medium-low speed to incorporate.

7. Scrape down the sides of the bowl and mix at high speed for about 5 seconds,

just until the batter is completely mixed and smooth.

8. Use a large rubber spatula to fold in the cherries.

9. Divide the batter evenly among the paper-lined cups. Make the top of the batter as smooth as you can.

10. Bake for 25 minutes.

11. Allow the cupcakes to cool in the tins for 10 minutes, then remove from the tins and let cool completely on a wire rack.

12. While the cupcakes are cooling, make the Cherry Vanilla Buttercream.

TO FINISH THE CUPCAKES:

13. Use a large star tip to pipe an upward spiral of the buttercream on the cupcakes.

Note: If using frozen cherries, it is easier to dice them while they are frozen.

CHERRY VANILLA BUTTERCREAM

1⅓ cups plus 1 tablespoon sugar, divided

½ cup water

4 large egg whites

¼ teaspoon salt

1½ cups salted butter (3 sticks), removed from the refrigerator when you start the buttercream

2 teaspoons GF pure vanilla extract

1 cup pitted whole cherries (frozen or fresh) (see Note, next page)

1. Mix 1⅓ cups of the sugar and the water in a heavy saucepan. Put a candy thermometer in the sugar mixture and heat to 240°F without stirring.
2. Meanwhile, in a stand mixer using a whisk attachment, whisk the egg whites and salt at medium-high speed until frothy.
3. Add the remaining 1 tablespoon of sugar to the egg whites and whisk until soft peaks form. Turn the mixer off and let the egg whites sit until the sugar comes up to temperature.
4. When the sugar-water mixture reaches 240°F, with the mixer at medium speed, slowly drizzle the hot sugar mixture down the side of the bowl into the beaten egg whites.
5. After all the sugar is added, continue whisking the mixture until it is cool, about 10 minutes.
6. While the egg whites are whisking, cut the butter into tablespoon-size pieces.
7. In a blender or food processor, puree the cherries until smooth. (If using fresh cherries, add 1 tablespoon of sugar if the puree is not smooth enough, then continue blending until smooth.)

8. When the egg whites are cool, leave the mixer running at medium speed and add the butter, 1 tablespoon at a time, allowing enough time for each tablespoon of butter to incorporate after each addition, until all the butter is added.

9. Add the vanilla and mix to combine.

10. Switch to the paddle attachment and add the pureed cherries. Mix for an additional 1 or 2 minutes at medium-high speed until the air bubbles are out of the frosting and the frosting is silky smooth.

Note: If using frozen cherries, allow the cherries to come to room temperature before pureeing.

Lemon Blueberry Cupcake

lemon blueberry cupcakes

MAKES 24 CUPCAKES

This cupcake features a lemon cake with blueberries folded into the batter and is topped with Blueberry Buttercream. Its bright flavors are sure to bring a ray of sunshine to any occasion.

¾ cup salted butter (1½ sticks),
  room temperature

1¾ cups sugar

1 teaspoon GF pure vanilla extract

2 large eggs, room temperature

2 large egg whites, room temperature

Zest from 1 lemon

¼ cup lemon juice (about 1 lemon,
  juiced) (see Note, next page)

6 tablespoons buttermilk, room
  temperature

3 cups Artisan Gluten-Free Flour
  Blend (page 10)

2 teaspoons xanthan gum

2½ teaspoons GF baking powder

1 teaspoon GF baking soda

½ teaspoon salt

½ pint fresh blueberries (frozen can
  be used)

Blueberry Buttercream (recipe
  follows)

24 fresh blueberries

TO MAKE THE CUPCAKES:

1. Preheat the oven to 350°F. Line standard cupcake tins with paper liners.

2. With an electric mixer, cream together the butter and sugar until light and fluffy, then add the vanilla.

3. Add the eggs and egg whites one at a time, mixing to incorporate after each addition.

4. Add the zest, lemon juice, and buttermilk, and mix until combined.

5. In a separate bowl, combine the flour, xanthan gum, baking powder, baking soda, and salt, and mix with a whisk to "sift" the ingredients and break up any lumps.

6. Add the dry ingredients all at once to the sugar mixture and mix for about 10 seconds at medium-low speed to incorporate.

7. Scrape down the sides of the bowl and mix at high speed for about 5 seconds, just until the batter is completely mixed and smooth.

8. Fold in the ½ pint of blueberries.
9. Divide the batter evenly among the paper-lined cups. Make the top of the batter as smooth as you can.
10. Bake for 25 minutes.
11. Allow the cupcakes to cool in the tins for 10 minutes, then remove from the tins and let cool completely on a wire rack.
12. While the cupcakes are cooling, make the Blueberry Buttercream.

TO FINISH THE CUPCAKES:

13. Use a large star tip to pipe the Blueberry Buttercream on the cupcakes. Start at the edge of the cupcake, making many small stars, and move toward the center. Pipe additional smaller tiers to add height.
14. Garnish the top of each cupcake with one fresh blueberry.

Note: Be sure to zest the lemon first before juicing. Zesting an already-juiced lemon is nearly impossible!

BLUEBERRY BUTTERCREAM

1⅓ cups plus 1 tablespoon sugar, divided

½ cup water

4 large egg whites

¼ teaspoon salt

1½ cups salted butter (3 sticks), removed from the refrigerator when you start the buttercream

2 teaspoons GF pure vanilla extract

1 pint fresh blueberries, pureed

1. Mix 1⅓ cups of the sugar and the water in a heavy saucepan. Put a candy thermometer in the sugar mixture and heat to 240°F without stirring.
2. Meanwhile, in a stand mixer using the whisk attachment, whisk the egg whites and salt at medium-high speed until frothy.
3. Add the remaining 1 tablespoon of sugar to the egg whites and whisk until soft peaks form. Turn the mixer off and let the egg whites sit until the sugar comes up to temperature.
4. When the sugar mixture reaches 240°F, with the mixer at medium speed, slowly drizzle the hot sugar mixture down the side of the bowl into the beaten egg whites.
5. After all the sugar is added, continue whisking the mixture until it is cool, about 10 minutes.
6. While the egg whites are whisking, cut the butter into tablespoon-size pieces and puree the blueberries.

continued

7. When the egg whites are cool, leave the mixer running at medium speed and add the butter, 1 tablespoon at a time, allowing enough time for each tablespoon of butter to incorporate after each addition, until all the butter is added.

8. Add the vanilla and mix to combine.

9. Switch to the paddle attachment, add the pureed blueberries, and mix for an additional 1 to 2 minutes at medium-high speed until the air bubbles are out of the frosting and the frosting is silky smooth.

lemon poppy seed cupcakes

round the house we joke that this recipe is for a "muffcake" since it treads the line between a cupcake and a muffin. But although the flavors were inspired by a lemon poppy seed muffin, we've ported them over into a cupcake and topped it off with Lemon Glaze for some added sweetness and zip.

¾ cup salted butter (1½ sticks), room temperature

1¾ cups sugar

1 teaspoon GF pure vanilla extract

2 large eggs, room temperature

2 large egg whites, room temperature

Zest from 1 lemon

¼ cup lemon juice (about 1 lemon, juiced)

¼ cup plus 2 tablespoons buttermilk, room temperature

¼ cup poppy seeds

3 cups Artisan Gluten-Free Flour Blend (page 10)

2 teaspoons xanthan gum

2½ teaspoons GF baking powder

1 teaspoon GF baking soda

½ teaspoon salt

Lemon Glaze (recipe follows)

Zest from 1 lemon (see Note, next page)

TO MAKE THE CUPCAKES:

1. Preheat the oven to 350°F. Line standard cupcake tins with paper liners.

2. With an electric mixer, cream together the butter and sugar until light and fluffy, then add the vanilla.

3. Add the eggs and egg whites one at a time, mixing to incorporate after each addition.

4. Add the zest from 1 lemon, lemon juice, buttermilk, and poppy seeds, and mix until combined.

5. In a separate bowl, combine the flour, xanthan gum, baking powder, baking soda, and salt, and mix with a whisk to "sift" the ingredients and break up any lumps.

6. Add the dry ingredients all at once to the sugar mixture and mix for about 10 seconds at medium-low speed to incorporate.

7. Scrape down the sides of the bowl and mix at high speed for about 5 seconds,

just until the batter is completely mixed and smooth.

8. Divide the batter evenly among the paper-lined cups. Make the top of the batter as smooth as you can.

9. Bake for 25 minutes.

10. Allow the cupcakes to cool in the tins for 10 minutes, then remove from the tins and let cool completely on a wire rack.

11. While the cupcakes are cooling, make the Lemon Glaze.

TO FINISH THE CUPCAKES:

12. Drizzle each cupcake with the Lemon Glaze, using enough so that a small amount spills over the edges.

13. Garnish with zest from 1 lemon.

Note: For the garnish, it is easiest to use a Microplane grater and zest the lemon directly over the cupcakes.

LEMON GLAZE

2 cups confectioners' sugar
¼ cup lemon juice

In a small bowl, mix the confectioners' sugar and lemon juice until the sugar is fully dissolved and the glaze is smooth. Use immediately.

Orange Cranberry Cupcake

orange cranberry cupcakes

Orange and cranberry is a flavor combination we've loved for years. We often make an orange-cranberry sorbet, and the cranberry relish we make every year for Thanksgiving has orange in it as well. Why not carry these flavors over into a cupcake? This recipe features a cranberry-flecked orange cupcake topped with a ring of Cream Cheese Frosting and a dollop of Orange Cranberry Relish.

¾ cup salted butter (1½ sticks), room temperature

1¾ cups sugar

1 teaspoon GF pure orange extract

2 large eggs, room temperature

2 large egg whites, room temperature

Zest from 2 oranges

½ cup orange juice (about 1 large navel orange, juiced) (see Note, next page)

¼ cup plus 2 tablespoons buttermilk, room temperature

1½ cups fresh whole cranberries, chopped

3 cups Artisan Gluten-Free Flour Blend (page 10)

2 teaspoons xanthan gum

2½ teaspoons GF baking powder

1 teaspoon GF baking soda

½ teaspoon salt

Cream Cheese Frosting (recipe follows)

Orange Cranberry Relish (recipe follows)

TO MAKE THE CUPCAKES:

1. Preheat the oven to 350°F. Line standard cupcake tins with paper liners.

2. With an electric mixer, cream together the butter and sugar until light and fluffy, then add the orange extract.

3. Add the eggs and egg whites one at a time, mixing to incorporate after each addition.

4. Add the zest, orange juice, buttermilk, and cranberries, and mix until combined.

5. In a separate bowl, combine the flour, xanthan gum, baking powder, baking soda, and salt, and mix with a whisk to "sift" the ingredients and break up any lumps.

6. Add the dry ingredients all at once to the sugar mixture and mix for about

10 seconds at medium-low speed to incorporate.

7. Scrape down the sides of the bowl and mix at high speed for about 5 seconds, just until the batter is completely mixed and smooth.

8. Divide the batter evenly among the paper-lined cups. Make the top of the batter as smooth as you can.

9. Bake for 25 minutes.

10. Allow the cupcakes to cool in the tins for 10 minutes, then remove from the tins and let cool completely on a wire rack.

11. While the cupcakes are cooling, make the Cream Cheese Frosting and the Orange Cranberry Relish.

TO FINISH THE CUPCAKES:

12. Use a large star tip to pipe rosettes of Cream Cheese Frosting around the edges of the cupcakes.

13. Center 1 heaping teaspoon of the Orange Cranberry Relish in the middle of the frosting.

Note: Be sure to zest the orange first before juicing. Zesting an already-juiced orange is nearly impossible!

CREAM CHEESE FROSTING

6 ounces cream cheese, room temperature
½ cup salted butter (1 stick), room temperature
2 cups confectioners' sugar
1 teaspoons GF pure vanilla extract

1. With an electric mixer, cream together the cream cheese and butter until completely incorporated.
2. Add the confectioners' sugar and vanilla, and mix until smooth and of spreading consistency. (Additional confectioners' sugar can be added, if needed, to make a thicker frosting.)

ORANGE CRANBERRY RELISH

1½ cups whole fresh cranberries
½ large navel orange with the rind, cut into pieces

Combine the cranberries and orange in a food processor and pulse until the fruit becomes a fine relish but is not a paste or puree.

piña colada cupcakes

MAKES 24 CUPCAKES

Whether served on a hot, sunny summer day or in the dead of winter to remind us of warm tropical getaways, this cupcake fits the bill. Based on the traditional flavor combo of its namesake drink, we take a fresh pineapple cupcake and top it with Coconut Frosting, flaked coconut, and a wedge of fresh pineapple.

½ cup plus 1 tablespoon salted butter (1 stick plus 1 tablespoon), room temperature

1¼ cups sugar

1½ teaspoons GF pure vanilla extract

3 large eggs, room temperature

¾ cup buttermilk, room temperature

¾ cup fresh pineapple puree (fresh-cut pineapple pulsed in a food processor or blender)

1½ cups fresh pineapple, diced small

2¼ cups Artisan Gluten-Free Flour Blend (page 10)

1½ teaspoons xanthan gum

2 teaspoons GF baking powder

¾ teaspoon GF baking soda

¾ teaspoon salt

Coconut Frosting (recipe follows)

½ cup sweetened flaked coconut

Fresh pineapple, cut into 24 small wedges

24 mini umbrellas (optional, but fun!)

TO MAKE THE CUPCAKES:

1. Preheat the oven to 350°F. Line standard cupcake tins with paper liners.

2. With an electric mixer, cream together the butter and sugar until light and fluffy, then add the vanilla.

3. Add the eggs one at a time, mixing to incorporate after each addition.

4. Add the buttermilk and mix until combined.

5. Add the pineapple puree and diced pineapple, and mix just to incorporate.

6. In a separate bowl, combine the flour, xanthan gum, baking powder, baking soda, and salt, and mix with a whisk to "sift" the ingredients and break up any lumps.

7. Add the dry ingredients all at once to the sugar mixture and mix for about 10 seconds at medium-low speed to incorporate.

8. Scrape down the sides of the bowl and mix at high speed for about 5 seconds,

just until the batter is completely mixed and smooth.

9. Divide the batter evenly among the paper-lined cups. Make the top of the batter as smooth as you can.

10. Bake for 25 minutes.

11. Allow the cupcakes to cool in the tins for 10 minutes, then remove from the tins and let cool completely on a wire rack.

12. While the cupcakes are cooling, make the Coconut Frosting.

TO FINISH THE CUPCAKES:

13. Use a small palette knife to spread the Coconut Frosting on top of the cupcakes.

14. Garnish with the flaked coconut, a wedge of pineapple, and a mini umbrella.

COCONUT FROSTING

¾ cup salted butter (1½ sticks), room temperature
3 cups confectioners' sugar
½ cup plus 1 tablespoon coconut cream (*not* coconut milk)
2 teaspoons heavy cream

Cream together the butter, confectioners' sugar, coconut cream, and heavy cream until light and fluffy. (If the frosting is too thick, add additional heavy cream 1 teaspoon at a time until you have the desired consistency.)

very strawberry cupcakes

Every year there seems to be some sweet spot in the calendar when strawberries are in season, abundant, inexpensive, and, best of all, fresh. They're sweet and juicy and vibrantly red. It's during those times when we think about this cupcake, which truly shines when the fruit that makes up its soul is at its best. Strawberries folded into the cake batter, Strawberry Frosting, and a fresh strawberry garnish help this cupcake live up to its apropos name.

¾ cup salted butter (1½ sticks), room temperature

1½ cups sugar

2 teaspoons GF pure vanilla extract

4 large eggs, room temperature

1 cup buttermilk, room temperature

1 quart strawberries, hulled and quartered

3¼ cups Artisan Gluten-Free Flour Blend (page 10)

2 teaspoons xanthan gum

2½ teaspoons GF baking powder

1 teaspoon GF baking soda

½ teaspoon salt

Strawberry Frosting (recipe follows)

4 to 6 strawberries, sliced

TO MAKE THE CUPCAKES:

1. Preheat the oven to 350°F. Line standard cupcake tins with paper liners.

2. With an electric mixer, cream together the butter and sugar until light and fluffy, then add the vanilla extract.

3. Add the eggs one at a time, mixing to incorporate after each addition.

4. Add the buttermilk and 1 quart of strawberries, and mix until combined.

5. In a separate bowl, combine the flour, xanthan gum, baking powder, baking soda, and salt, and mix with a whisk to "sift" the ingredients and break up any lumps.

6. Add the dry ingredients all at once to the sugar mixture and mix for about 10 seconds at medium-low speed to incorporate.

7. Scrape down the sides of the bowl and mix at high speed for about 5 seconds, just until the batter is completely mixed and smooth.

8. Divide the batter evenly among the paper-lined cups. Make the top of the batter as smooth as you can.

9. Bake for 25 minutes.

10. Allow the cupcakes to cool in the tins for 10 minutes, then remove from the tins and let cool completely on a wire rack.

11. While the cupcakes are cooling, make the Strawberry Frosting.

TO FINISH THE CUPCAKES:

12. Use a large star tip to pipe an upward spiral of frosting on the cupcakes.

13. Garnish with one strawberry slice on top.

STRAWBERRY FROSTING

1 cup salted butter (2 sticks), room temperature
4 cups confectioners' sugar
¼ cup pureed strawberries
1 teaspoon GF pure vanilla extract

Cream together the butter, confectioners' sugar, strawberries, and vanilla until light and fluffy.

Very Strawberry Cupcake

mango mania cupcakes

If you're looking for a cupcake that shouts "fresh tropical fruit flavor," look no further! From a mango-infused cupcake, to a Mango Buttercream, to a fresh mango garnish, this refreshing cupcake is mango to the max.

3/4 cup salted butter (1½ sticks), room temperature

1¾ cups sugar

2 teaspoons GF pure vanilla extract

2 large eggs, room temperature

2 large egg whites, room temperature

1 cup milk

¼ cup sour cream

3 cups Artisan Gluten-Free Flour Blend (page 10)

2 teaspoons xanthan gum

2½ teaspoons GF baking powder

1 teaspoon GF baking soda

½ teaspoon salt

1 mango, diced small (see Note, next page)

Mango Buttercream (recipe follows)

1 mango, sliced

TO MAKE THE CUPCAKES:

1. Preheat the oven to 350°F. Line standard cupcake tins with paper liners.

2. With an electric mixer, cream together the butter and sugar until fluffy, then add the vanilla.

3. Add the eggs and egg whites one at a time, mixing to incorporate after each addition.

4. Add the milk and sour cream, and mix until combined.

5. In a separate bowl, combine the flour, xanthan gum, baking powder, baking soda, and salt, and mix with a whisk to "sift" the ingredients and break up any lumps.

6. Add the dry ingredients all at once to the sugar mixture and mix for about 10 seconds at medium-low speed to incorporate.

7. Scrape down the sides of the bowl and mix at high speed for about 5 seconds, just until the batter is completely mixed and smooth.

8. Use a large rubber spatula to fold in 1 diced mango.

9. Divide the batter evenly among the paper-lined cups. Make the top of the batter as smooth as you can.
10. Bake for 25 minutes.
11. Allow the cupcakes to cool in the tin for 10 minutes, then remove from the tins and let cool completely on a wire rack.
12. While the cupcakes are cooling, make the Mango Buttercream.

TO FINISH THE CUPCAKES:
13. Use a petal tip to pipe Mango Buttercream on the cupcakes.
14. Garnish with the fresh sliced mango.

Note: Be sure the mangos are ripe. When you press on the flesh, the mangos should give slightly, but the skin should not be wrinkly. If you cannot find fresh mangos, canned or jarred mangos can be substituted for the diced mango in the batter and the pureed mango in the buttercream.

MANGO BUTTERCREAM

1⅓ cups plus 1 tablespoon sugar, divided
½ cup water
4 large egg whites
¼ teaspoon salt
1½ cups salted butter (3 sticks), removed from the refrigerator when you start the buttercream
2 teaspoons GF pure vanilla extract
½ cup mango puree (about ½ mango)

1. Mix 1⅓ cups of the sugar and the water in a heavy saucepan. Put a candy thermometer in the sugar mixture and heat to 240°F without stirring.

2. Meanwhile, in a stand mixer using a whisk attachment, whisk the egg whites and salt at medium-high speed until frothy.

3. Add the remaining 1 tablespoon of sugar to the egg whites and whisk until soft peaks form. Turn the mixer off and let the egg whites sit until the sugar comes up to temperature.

4. When the sugar mixture reaches 240°F, with the mixer at medium speed, slowly drizzle the hot sugar mixture down the side of the bowl into the beaten egg whites.

5. After all the sugar is added, continue whisking the mixture until it is cool, about 10 minutes.

6. While the egg whites are whisking, cut the butter into tablespoon-size pieces.

continued

7. When the egg whites are cool, leave the mixer running at medium speed and add the butter, 1 tablespoon at a time, allowing enough time for each tablespoon of butter to incorporate after each addition, until all the butter is added.

8. Add the vanilla and mix to combine.

9. Switch to the paddle attachment and add the pureed mango. Mix for an additional 1 or 2 minutes at medium-high speed until the air bubbles are out of the frosting and the frosting is silky smooth.

nutty

Tree nuts such as almonds, walnuts, and hazelnuts give both flavor and texture to this group of cupcakes. With nuts in the cake, in the frosting, or on the frosting (or some combination thereof), channel your inner squirrel and let the nut lover in you go to town on these nutty cupcakes.

Almond Addiction Cupcake

almond addiction cupcakes

MAKES 24 CUPCAKES

Almond is Kelli's favorite cake flavor, so there's no way we could write a cupcake cookbook without including this recipe. It starts with a from-scratch Almond Paste we use to make an almond cake and an Almond Buttercream, and we finish it off with some sliced almonds on top. If you love almonds even half as much as Kelli does, what's not to love about this cupcake?

2 cups blanched almonds

2½ cups Artisan Gluten-Free Flour Blend (page 10)

1 teaspoon xanthan gum

2 teaspoons GF baking powder

1 teaspoon GF baking soda

½ teaspoon salt

1¼ cups salted butter (2½ sticks), room temperature

1½ cups sugar

½ cup Almond Paste (recipe follows)

2 teaspoons GF pure almond extract

6 large eggs, room temperature

Almond Buttercream (recipe follows)

Sliced almonds

1. First, make the Almond Paste.

TO MAKE THE CUPCAKES:

2. Preheat the oven to 350°F. Line standard cupcake tins with paper liners.

3. Place the blanched almonds in a food processor and process until the almonds are ground very fine (almost like a flour).

4. Add the flour, xanthan gum, baking powder, baking soda, and salt, and pulse to combine. Set aside.

5. With an electric mixer, cream together the butter and sugar until light and fluffy.

6. Add the Almond Paste and mix at medium speed until smooth, then stir in the almond extract.

7. Add the eggs one at a time, mixing to incorporate after each addition.

8. Add the dry ingredients (from the food processor) all at once to the sugar mixture and mix for about 10 seconds at medium-low speed to incorporate.

9. Scrape down the sides of the bowl and mix at high speed for about 5 seconds, just until the batter is completely mixed and smooth.

10. Divide the batter evenly among the paper-lined cups. Make the top of the batter as smooth as you can.
11. Bake for 25–30 minutes, until a toothpick inserted into the center of one cupcake comes out clean.
12. Allow the cupcakes to cool in the tins for 10 minutes, then remove from the tins and let cool completely on a wire rack.
13. While the cupcakes are cooling, make the Almond Buttercream.

TO FINISH THE CUPCAKES:
14. Use a palette knife to spread the Almond Buttercream on the cupcakes.
15. Garnish with the sliced almonds.

ALMOND PASTE

10 ounces whole blanched almonds (about 2 cups)
⅔ cup sugar
¼ cup water
1 tablespoon GF pure almond extract

1. Place the almonds in a food processor and process until the almonds are ground very fine (almost like a flour).
2. Add the sugar and pulse to combine.
3. Add the water and almond extract, and process the mixture until it is a smooth paste consistency.

Note: You can also use store-bought almond paste, but if so, *please* read the ingredients label. Not all brands are gluten-free. Some are made with wheat. The Solo brand is widely available and generally accepted as gluten-free.

ALMOND BUTTERCREAM

1⅓ cups plus 1 tablespoon sugar, divided

½ cup water

4 large egg whites

¼ teaspoon salt

1½ cups salted butter (3 sticks), removed from the refrigerator when you start the buttercream

2 teaspoons GF pure almond extract

½ cup Almond Paste (recipe on previous page)

1. Mix 1⅓ cups of the sugar and the water in a heavy saucepan. Put a candy thermometer in the sugar mixture and heat to 240°F without stirring.
2. Meanwhile, in a stand mixer using the whisk attachment, whisk the egg whites and salt at medium-high speed until frothy.
3. Add the remaining 1 tablespoon of sugar to the egg whites and whisk until soft peaks form. Turn the mixer off and let the egg whites sit until the sugar comes up to temperature.
4. When sugar mixture reaches 240°F, with the mixer at medium speed, slowly drizzle the hot sugar mixture down the side of the bowl into the beaten egg whites.
5. After all the sugar is added, continue whisking the mixture until it is cool, about 10 minutes.
6. While the egg whites are whisking, cut the butter into tablespoon-size pieces.
7. When the egg whites are cool, leave the mixer running at medium speed and add the butter, 1 tablespoon at a time, allowing enough time for each tablespoon of butter to incorporate after each addition, until all the butter is added.
8. Add the almond extract and mix to combine.
9. Switch to the paddle attachment, add the Almond Paste, and mix at medium speed for an additional 1 to 2 minutes until the air bubbles are out of the frosting and the frosting is thoroughly mixed and silky smooth.

hazelnutty cupcakes

MAKES 24 CUPCAKES

This recipe is like a cupcake version of Ferrero Rocher chocolate hazelnut truffles (which, sadly, are not gluten-free . . . all the more reason to love these cupcakes, which are!). We start with a quasi-sponge cake that contains oodles of lightly roasted, finely ground hazelnuts, then top it off with a rich Chocolate Buttercream and garnish with crushed hazelnuts. One bite and we swear you'll go to hazelnut heaven.

1½ cups salted butter (3 sticks)

1½ cups Roasted Hazelnuts (recipe follows)

2 cups confectioners' sugar

½ cup Artisan Gluten-Free Flour Blend (page 10)

¾ teaspoon xanthan gum

9 large egg whites

4½ tablespoons sugar

1 tablespoon GF pure vanilla extract

Chocolate Buttercream (recipe follows)

½ cup Roasted Hazelnuts

1. First, make the Roasted Hazelnuts.

TO MAKE THE CUPCAKES:

2. Preheat the oven to 350°F. Line standard cupcake tins with paper liners.

3. Melt the butter in a saucepan over medium heat until the butter is golden brown, 8 to 10 minutes. Remove from the heat and set aside.

4. Meanwhile, place the 1½ cups of Roasted Hazelnuts in a food processor and process until the nuts are finely ground.

5. Add the confectioners' sugar and process for 1 minute.

6. Add the flour and xanthan gum and pulse to combine. Set aside.

7. In the bowl of an electric mixer using the whisk attachment, beat the egg whites until foamy.

8. Add the sugar and whisk at medium-high speed until stiff peaks form.

9. Add the vanilla and whisk to combine.

10. Use a rubber spatula to fold in the hazelnut mixture from the food processor. Add the melted browned butter (from step 2) and fold in just to incorporate.

11. Divide the batter evenly among the paper-lined cups.

12. Bake for 30 minutes or until a toothpick inserted in the center of one cupcake comes out clean.
13. Allow the cupcakes to cool in the tins for 10 minutes, then remove from the tins and let cool completely on a wire rack.
14. While the cupcakes are cooling, make the Chocolate Buttercream.

TO FINISH THE CUPCAKES:
15. Put the ½ cup of Roasted Hazelnuts in a zip-top bag and crush with a rolling pin.
16. Use a small palette knife to spread the Chocolate Buttercream on the cupcakes.
17. Garnish with the crushed Roasted Hazelnuts.

ROASTED HAZELNUTS

2 cups whole hazelnuts, shells removed

1. Preheat the oven to 350°F.
2. Place the nuts in a single layer on a cookie sheet and roast for 12 to 15 minutes, until the nuts are fragrant. (Be careful not to leave them in for too long or they will burn.)
3. Place the nuts in a kitchen towel and wrap them up for about 5 minutes to self-steam.
4. Roll the nuts in the towel to remove the skins. You may need to rub individual nuts by hand to remove any remaining skin. (Although not strictly necessary, the more skin you can remove the better, since the skin imparts an undesirable bitterness.)

Hazelnutty Cupcake

CHOCOLATE BUTTERCREAM

1⅓ cups plus 1 tablespoon sugar, divided

½ cup water

4 large egg whites

¼ teaspoon salt

1½ cups salted butter (3 sticks), removed from the refrigerator when you start the buttercream

2 teaspoons GF pure vanilla extract

8 ounces semi-sweet chocolate, melted and cooled
(about 1⅓ cups chips or pieces)

1. Mix 1⅓ cups of the sugar and the water in a heavy saucepan. Put a candy thermometer in the sugar mixture and heat to 240°F without stirring.
2. Meanwhile, in a stand mixer using the whisk attachment, whisk the egg whites and salt at medium-high speed until frothy.
3. Add the remaining 1 tablespoon of sugar to the egg whites and whisk until soft peaks form. Turn the mixer off and let the egg whites sit until the sugar comes up to temperature.
4. When the sugar mixture reaches 240°F, with the mixer at medium speed, slowly drizzle the hot sugar mixture down the side of the bowl into the beaten egg whites.
5. After all the sugar is added, continue whisking the mixture until it is cool, about 10 minutes.
6. While the egg whites are whisking, cut the butter into tablespoon-size pieces.
7. When the egg whites are cool, leave the mixer running at medium speed and add the butter, 1 tablespoon at a time, allowing enough time for each tablespoon of butter to incorporate after each addition, until all the butter is added.
8. Add the vanilla and chocolate, and mix to combine.
9. Switch to the paddle attachment and mix for an additional 1 to 2 minutes at medium-high speed until the air bubbles are out of the frosting and the frosting is silky smooth.

Pistachio Cupcake

pistachio cupcakes

As much as Kelli loves almond, she also loves pistachio. It should come as no surprise, then, that her favorite flavor of ice cream is pistachio, which is often an almond-flavored ice cream with pistachio nuts throughout. We modeled our cupcake on that formula. It features a pistachio and almond cake topped with a pistachio and almond buttercream and garnished with some crushed/chopped pistachios. The likeness to pistachio ice cream (if it existed in an alternate dimension as a cupcake, of course) is remarkable.

1 cup shelled unsalted pistachios
(see Note, next page)

¾ cup salted butter (1½ sticks),
room temperature

1¾ cups packed brown sugar

2 teaspoons GF pure almond
extract

4 large eggs, room temperature

1¼ cups buttermilk, room temperature

3 cups Artisan Gluten-Free Flour
Blend (page 10)

2 teaspoons xanthan gum

2½ teaspoons GF baking powder

1 teaspoon GF baking soda

½ teaspoon salt

Pistachio Buttercream (recipe
follows)

½ cup shelled unsalted pistachios

TO MAKE THE CUPCAKES:

1. Preheat the oven to 350°F. Line standard cupcake tins with paper liners.

2. In a food processor, pulse the 1 cup of pistachios until finely ground. Set aside.

3. With an electric mixer, cream together the butter and brown sugar until light and fluffy, then add the almond extract.

4. Add the eggs one at a time, mixing to incorporate after each addition.

5. Add the buttermilk and ground pistachios, and mix until combined.

6. In a separate bowl, combine the flour, xanthan gum, baking powder, baking soda, and salt, and mix with a whisk to "sift" the ingredients and break up any lumps.

7. Add the dry ingredients all at once to the sugar mixture and mix for about 10 seconds at medium-low speed to incorporate.

8. Scrape down the sides of the bowl and mix at high speed for about 5 seconds, just until the batter is completely mixed and smooth.

9. Divide the batter evenly among the paper-lined cups. Make the top of the batter as smooth as you can.

10. Bake for 25 minutes.

11. Allow the cupcakes to cool in the tins for 10 minutes, then remove from the tins and let cool completely on a wire rack.

12. While the cupcakes are cooling, make the Pistachio Buttercream.

TO FINISH THE CUPCAKES:

13. Put the ½ cup shelled pistachios in a zip-top bag and use a rolling pin to crush into small pieces.

14. Use a small palette knife to spread a generous portion of Pistachio Buttercream on the cupcakes.

15. Garnish with the crushed pistachios.

Note: If you can only find salted pistachios, leave the salt out of both the cake and buttercream.

PISTACHIO BUTTERCREAM

1 cup shelled unsalted pistachios (see Note, previous page)

1½ cups salted butter (3 sticks), removed from the refrigerator when you start the buttercream

1⅓ cups plus 1 tablespoon sugar, divided

½ cup water

4 large egg whites

¼ teaspoon salt

2 teaspoons GF pure almond extract

1. In the food processor, pulse the pistachios until they are very fine.
2. Cut the butter into pieces, add to the food processor, and puree until the mixture is completely mixed and a uniform green color.
3. Transfer the pistachio butter to an airtight container and place in the refrigerator. (The mixture can be done up to a few days in advance of making the buttercream, though it is also easily done *a la minute*.)
4. Mix 1⅓ cups of the sugar and the water in a heavy saucepan. Put a candy thermometer in the sugar mixture and heat to 240°F without stirring.
5. Meanwhile, in a stand mixer using the whisk attachment, whisk the egg whites and salt at medium-high speed until frothy.
6. Add the remaining 1 tablespoon of sugar to the egg whites and whisk until soft peaks form. Turn the mixer off and let the egg whites sit until the sugar comes up to temperature.
7. When the sugar-water mixture reaches 240°F, with the mixer at medium speed, slowly drizzle the hot sugar mixture down the side of the bowl into the beaten egg whites.

continued

8. After all the sugar is added, continue whisking the mixture until it is cool, about 10 minutes.
9. While the egg whites are whisking, pull the pistachio butter out of the refrigerator and cut into tablespoon-size pieces.
10. When the egg whites are cool, leave the mixer running at medium speed and add the pistachio butter, 1 tablespoon at a time, allowing enough time for each tablespoon to incorporate after each addition, until all the butter is added.
11. Add the almond extract and mix to combine.
12. Switch to the paddle attachment and mix for an additional 1 to 2 minutes at medium-high speed until the air bubbles are out of the frosting and the frosting is silky smooth.

sweet potato walnut cupcakes

MAKES 24 CUPCAKES

Sweet potato works surprisingly well in baking. It has a subtle flavor, and it lends moisture and a tender crumb to cakes. Our cupcake is delicious in its own right, but if you're looking for another reason to make it, it's also a great way to use up leftover sweet potatoes from dinner. The recipe calls for mashed sweet potatoes. We typically peel, quarter, and steam our sweet potatoes, but they can also be boiled. The butter–brown sugar–walnut topping adds major flavor and takes the subtle sweet potato to new heights.

½ cup salted butter (1 stick), room temperature

1 cup packed brown sugar

1 cup sugar

2 teaspoons GF pure vanilla extract

4 large eggs, room temperature

¾ cup sour cream

1 cup mashed sweet potato

2½ cups Artisan Gluten-Free Flour Blend (page 10)

2 teaspoons xanthan gum

1 tablespoon GF baking powder

1 teaspoon GF baking soda

½ teaspoon salt

2 teaspoons ground cinnamon

½ teaspoon ground ginger

½ teaspoon ground allspice

Walnut Topping (recipe follows)

1. First, make the Walnut Topping.

TO MAKE THE CUPCAKES:

2. Preheat the oven to 350°F. Line standard cupcake tins with paper liners.

3. With an electric mixer, cream together the butter, brown sugar, and sugar until light and fluffy, then add the vanilla.

4. Add the eggs one at a time, mixing to incorporate after each addition.

5. Add the sour cream and sweet potato, and mix until combined.

6. In a separate bowl, combine the flour, xanthan gum, baking powder, baking soda, salt, cinnamon, ginger, and allspice, and mix with a whisk to "sift" the ingredients and break up any lumps.

7. Add the dry ingredients all at once to the sugar mixture and mix for about

10 seconds at medium-low speed to incorporate.

8. Scrape down the sides of the bowl and mix at high speed for about 5 seconds, just until the batter is completely mixed and smooth.

9. Divide the batter evenly among the paper-lined cups. Make the top of the batter as smooth as you can.

10. Sprinkle the Walnut Topping evenly among the cupcakes.

11. Bake for 25 minutes.

12. Allow the cupcakes to cool completely in the tins.

TO FINISH THE CUPCAKES:

13. Simply remove from the tins and enjoy.

WALNUT TOPPING

1 cup packed brown sugar
½ cup salted butter (1 stick)
2 teaspoons ground cinnamon
1 cup chopped walnuts

1. Combine the brown sugar, butter, cinnamon, and walnuts in a medium saucepan and heat over medium-high heat, stirring occasionally, until the mixture boils and the sugar dissolves.

2. Remove from the heat and set aside.

Sweet Potato
Walnut Cupcakes

chocoholic

Chocolate lovers, rejoice! These cupcakes feature choco-late, chocolate, and more chocolate. From Chocolate Mint and Chocolate Raspberry, to Mocha, S'mores, and more, their flavors range from mildly to intensely chocolaty. Even the most impassioned chocoholic will feel satisfied.

Chocolate Mint Cupcake

chocolate mint cupcakes

Like a cupcake version of an Andes Crème de Menthe Thin or a Thin Mint, this recipe pairs a chocolate mint cupcake with Mint Whipped Cream. The chocolate and mint are in perfect balance; neither overpowers the other. The Mint Whipped Cream is light and airy; shaved semi-sweet chocolate and mint leaves make a flavorful garnish that complements the main flavors of the cake and the whipped cream.

1 cup salted butter (2 sticks)

1 cup water

½ cup unsweetened cocoa powder (regular or dark)

2 cups sugar

2 large eggs

1 cup sour cream

2 teaspoons GF mint extract

2½ cups Artisan Gluten-Free Flour Blend (page 10)

2 teaspoons xanthan gum

1½ teaspoons GF baking powder

1½ teaspoons GF baking soda

½ teaspoon salt

Mint Whipped Cream (recipe follows)

1 ounce semi-sweet chocolate, bar form

24 sprigs fresh mint

TO MAKE THE CUPCAKES:

1. Preheat the oven to 350°F. Line standard cupcake tins with paper liners.

2. Heat the butter, water, and cocoa over medium heat in a saucepan until the butter is melted.

3. Meanwhile, put the sugar in a mixing bowl. Add the butter-cocoa mixture to the sugar and mix at low speed for about 5 minutes, or until the mixture is cool.

4. Add the eggs one at a time, mixing to incorporate after each addition.

5. Add the sour cream and mint extract, mix to incorporate, and scrape down the sides of the bowl.

6. In a separate bowl, combine the flour, xanthan gum, baking powder, baking soda, and salt, and mix with a whisk to "sift" the ingredients and break up any lumps.

7. Add the dry ingredients to the cocoa-sour cream mixture and mix for about 10 seconds at medium-low speed to incorporate.

8. Scrape down the sides of the bowl and mix for an additional 5 seconds at high speed, just until everything is mixed and smooth.

9. Divide the batter evenly among the paper-lined cups. Make the top of the batter as smooth as you can.

10. Bake for 25 minutes.

11. Allow the cupcakes to cool in the tins for 10 minutes, then remove from the tins and let cool completely on a wire rack.

12. While the cupcakes are cooling, make the Mint Whipped Cream.

TO FINISH THE CUPCAKES:

13. Use a large star tip to pipe a spiral of Mint Whipped Cream on the cupcakes.

14. Use a Microplane grater to shave semi-sweet chocolate over the whipped cream.

15. Garnish each cupcake with a sprig of fresh mint.

MINT WHIPPED CREAM

2 cups heavy cream
2 tablespoons confectioners' sugar
2 teaspoons GF mint extract

1. Chill a metal mixing bowl and a whisk or eggbeaters in the freezer for 5 minutes.

2. Pour the cream into the cold bowl and whisk until it starts to thicken.

3. Add the confectioners' sugar and mint extract, and whisk until soft peaks form. Do not over-mix or the over-whipped cream will take on a curdled appearance. (If this does happen, it's purely a cosmetic issue and won't affect the taste of the whipped cream.)

chocolate peanut butter cupcakes

MAKES 24 CUPCAKES

As if a chocolate cupcake with peanut butter frosting weren't enough, this cupcake includes a prize in the center—a Reese's miniature chocolate peanut butter cup.

1 cup salted butter (2 sticks)

1 cup water

½ cup unsweetened cocoa powder (regular or dark)

2 cups sugar

2 large eggs

1 cup sour cream

1 teaspoon GF pure vanilla extract

2½ cups Artisan Gluten-Free Flour Blend (page 10)

2 teaspoons xanthan gum

1½ teaspoons GF baking powder

1 ½ teaspoons GF baking soda

½ teaspoon salt

24 miniature peanut butter cups

Peanut Butter Frosting (recipe follows)

12 miniature peanut butter cups

TO MAKE THE CUPCAKES:

1. Preheat the oven to 350°F. Line standard cupcake tins with paper liners.

2. Heat the butter, water, and cocoa over medium heat in a saucepan until the butter is melted.

3. Meanwhile, put the sugar in a mixing bowl. Add the butter-cocoa mixture and mix at low speed for about 5 minutes, or until the mixture is cool.

4. Add the eggs one at a time, mixing to incorporate after each addition.

5. Add the sour cream and vanilla, mix to incorporate, and scrape down the sides of the bowl.

6. In a separate bowl, combine the flour, xanthan gum, baking powder, baking soda, and salt, and mix with a whisk to "sift" the ingredients and break up any lumps.

7. Add the dry ingredients to the cocoa-sour cream mixture and mix for about 10 seconds at medium-low speed to incorporate.

8. Scrape down the sides of the bowl and mix for an additional 5 seconds at high speed, just until everything is mixed and smooth.

9. Divide the batter evenly among the paper-lined cups.
10. Unwrap the 24 peanut butter cups and press one down into the center of each cupcake; cover with batter to fully enclose the peanut butter cup. Make the top of the batter as smooth as you can.
11. Bake for 25 minutes.
12. Allow the cupcakes to cool in the tins for 10 minutes, then remove from the tins and let cool completely on a wire rack.
13. While the cupcakes are cooling, make the Peanut Butter Frosting.

TO FINISH THE CUPCAKES:
14. Use a small palette knife to spread the Peanut Butter Frosting on each cupcake.
15. Unwrap the remaining 12 peanut butter cups, cut each in half, and garnish each cupcake with ½ peanut butter cup.

PEANUT BUTTER FROSTING

2 cups natural peanut butter (see Note)
1 cup salted butter, room temperature
3 cups confectioners' sugar
6 tablespoons heavy cream
½ teaspoon salt

1. Cream together the peanut butter and butter at medium-high speed until completely incorporated.
2. Add the confectioners' sugar, cream, and salt, and mix at medium-high speed until fluffy. (Add 1 teaspoon of additional cream at a time if the frosting is too thick.)

Note: This recipe calls for natural peanut butter, which means un- or lightly sweetened as well as un- or lightly salted. If you opt to use a standard peanut butter such as Skippy or Jif, omit the salt from the frosting.

Chocolate Peanut Butter Cupcake

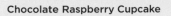
Chocolate Raspberry Cupcake

chocolate raspberry cupcakes

MAKES 24 CUPCAKES

Surely chocolate-raspberry must fall into the category of divine flavor pairings. The bold chocolate flavor of the cupcake and whipped ganache combined with the sweet, fruity Raspberry Sauce (and topped with a fresh raspberry) is as at home in this cupcake as it is on the white china of the best fine dining restaurants.

1 cup salted butter (2 sticks)

1 cup water

½ cup unsweetened cocoa powder (regular or dark)

2 cups sugar

2 large eggs

1 cup sour cream

1 teaspoon GF pure vanilla extract

2½ cups Artisan Gluten-Free Flour Blend (page 10)

2 teaspoons xanthan gum

1½ teaspoons GF baking powder

1½ teaspoons GF baking soda

½ teaspoon salt

Whipped Chocolate Ganache (recipe follows)

Raspberry Sauce (recipe follows)

24 fresh raspberries

TO MAKE THE CUPCAKES:

1. Preheat the oven to 350°F. Line standard cupcake tins with paper liners.

2. Heat the butter, water, and cocoa over medium heat in a saucepan until the butter is melted.

3. Meanwhile, put the sugar in a mixing bowl. Add the butter-cocoa mixture to the sugar and mix at low speed for about 5 minutes, or until the mixture is cool.

4. Add the eggs one at a time, mixing to incorporate after each addition.

5. Add the sour cream and vanilla, mix to incorporate, and scrape down the sides of the bowl.

6. In a separate bowl, combine the flour, xanthan gum, baking powder, baking soda, and salt, and mix with a whisk to "sift" the ingredients and break up any lumps.

7. Add the dry ingredients to the cocoa-sour cream mixture and mix for about 10 seconds at medium-low speed to incorporate.

8. Scrape down the sides of the bowl and mix for an additional 5 seconds at high

speed, just until everything is mixed and smooth.

9. Divide the batter evenly among the paper-lined cups. Make the top of the batter as smooth as you can.

10. Bake for 25 minutes.

11. Allow the cupcakes to cool in the tins for 10 minutes, then remove from the tins and let cool completely on a wire rack.

12. While the cupcakes are cooling, prepare the Whipped Chocolate Ganache and the Raspberry Sauce.

TO FINISH THE CUPCAKES:

13. Use a small palette knife to spread Whipped Chocolate Ganache on top of each cupcake.

14. Use a pastry bag with a small open tip or a zip-top bag with a small bottom corner cut to drizzle Raspberry Sauce on top.

15. Garnish each cupcake with one fresh raspberry.

WHIPPED CHOCOLATE GANACHE

16 ounces bittersweet chocolate (about 2⅔ cups chocolate chips or pieces)
1½ cups heavy cream

1. Put the chocolate in a bowl.

2. Heat the heavy cream to a simmer in a saucepan.

3. Pour the cream over the chocolate and let sit for 1 minute.

4. Stir the chocolate and cream together until the chocolate melts completely. Let the ganache sit until it is completely cool. (If making more than 2 hours in advance, refrigerate the ganache and bring back to room temperature before use. This will result in a less shiny finished product.)

5. With an electric mixer, beat the cooled ganache at medium-high speed (use the paddle attachment on a stand mixer), scraping down the sides of the bowl frequently to incorporate all the chocolate. The chocolate with become lighter in color and the consistency of spreadable frosting.

RASPBERRY SAUCE

⅓ cup cool water
1½ teaspoons cornstarch
⅓ cup sugar
1 cup raspberries (fresh or frozen)

1. Mix the water and cornstarch in a saucepan.
2. Add the sugar and raspberries, and heat over medium-high heat until the mixture comes to a boil.
3. Boil for 2 minutes, stirring constantly until the sauce is clear and slightly thickened.
4. Remove from the heat. Use an immersion or standard blender to puree the mixture until smooth.
5. Strain the blended sauce through a fine mesh strainer to remove all the seeds.
6. Let cool to room temperature.

S'mores Cupcake

s'mores cupcakes

Who says a cupcake's place is in the kitchen? With this recipe, cupcakes head into the backcountry on a camping trip for a night spent 'round the campfire. An optional gluten-free Mini Blondie Cookie serves as the graham cracker, and a chocolate cupcake and torch-melted chocolate chips—plus toasted Marshmallow Frosting—complete the time-honored s'mores formula. If using the Mini Blondie Cookies, allow extra time to bake a batch of cookies first, before preparing the cupcakes.

1 cup salted butter (2 sticks)

1 cup water

½ cup unsweetened cocoa powder (regular or dark)

2 cups sugar

2 large eggs

1 cup sour cream

1 teaspoon GF pure vanilla extract

2½ cups Artisan Gluten-Free Flour Blend (page 10)

2 teaspoons xanthan gum

1½ teaspoons GF baking powder

1½ teaspoons GF baking soda

½ teaspoon salt

Marshmallow Frosting (recipe follows)

Mini Blondie Cookies (recipe follows), optional

1 cup semi-sweet chocolate chips

1. First, make the Mini Blondie Cookies, if using.

TO MAKE THE CUPCAKES:

2. Preheat the oven to 350°F. Line standard cupcake tins with paper liners.

3. Heat the butter, water, and cocoa over medium heat in a saucepan until the butter is melted.

4. Meanwhile, put the sugar in a mixing bowl. Add the butter-cocoa mixture and mix at low speed for about 5 minutes, or until the mixture is cool.

5. Add the eggs one at a time, mixing to incorporate after each addition.

6. Add the sour cream and vanilla, mix to incorporate, and scrape down the sides of the bowl.

7. In a separate bowl, combine the flour, xanthan gum, baking powder, baking

soda, and salt, and mix with a whisk to "sift" the ingredients and break up any lumps.

8. Add the dry ingredients to the cocoa–sour cream mixture and mix for about 10 seconds at medium-low speed to incorporate.

9. Scrape down the sides of the bowl and mix for an additional 5 seconds at high speed, just until everything is mixed and smooth.

10. Divide the batter evenly among the paper-lined cups. Make the top of the batter as smooth as you can.

11. Bake for 25 minutes.

12. Allow the cupcakes to cool in the tins for 10 minutes, then remove from the tins and let cool completely on a wire rack.

13. While the cupcakes are cooling, make the Marshmallow Frosting.

TO FINISH THE CUPCAKES:

14. Use a small palette knife to spread the Marshmallow Frosting on top of the cupcakes.

15. Optional step: Place one Mini Blondie Cookie on top of the frosting and spread additional frosting on top of the cookie.

16. Garnish with chocolate chips scattered over the frosting.

17. To toast the Marshmallow Frosting to a golden brown, use a kitchen torch and wave the flame back and forth a few inches away from the cupcake. Be careful not to burn the chocolate or ignite the marshmallow. As you near the lip of the cupcake's paper liner, point the flame upward to avoid burning the paper.

MINI BLONDIE COOKIES

½ cup salted butter (1 stick), room temperature
¼ cup plus 2 tablespoons sugar
¼ cup plus 2 tablespoons packed brown sugar
½ teaspoon GF pure vanilla extract
1 large egg
1¼ cups Artisan Gluten-Free Flour Blend (page 10)
1¼ teaspoons xanthan gum
½ teaspoon GF baking soda
¼ teaspoon salt

1. Preheat the oven to 375°F.
2. Cream together the butter, sugar, brown sugar, and vanilla until light and fluffy.
3. Add the egg and mix to incorporate.
4. Add the flour, xanthan gum, baking soda, and salt and mix until well blended.
5. Drop ½-teaspoon-size scoops of dough onto an ungreased cookie sheet 1 inch apart.
6. Bake for 6 to 8 minutes, until golden brown. Let the cookies rest for 2 minutes on the cookie sheet, then transfer to a wire rack to cool completely.

MARSHMALLOW FROSTING

1½ cups sugar
½ cup water
1 tablespoon corn syrup
2 large egg whites
1 teaspoon GF pure vanilla extract

1. With a handheld electric mixer, combine the sugar, water, corn syrup, and egg whites in a bowl.
2. Place the bowl over a saucepan of simmering water. Make sure the water is not touching the bottom of the bowl. Using the handheld electric mixer at medium-high speed, beat the ingredients in the bowl for 7 to 8 minutes, until the mixture is very thick and looks like gooey marshmallow.
3. Remove the bowl from the heat and add the vanilla.
4. Beat the mixture for 2 to 3 minutes, until it cools slightly and is very fluffy.

flourless chocolate cupcakes

MAKES 24 CUPCAKES

This naturally gluten-free cupcake is rich and decadent. The flourless chocolate cake and Poured Chocolate Ganache are a chocolate lover's dream; the fresh berries cut through with a pleasing sweetness.

Melted butter or nonstick cooking
　spray
½ cup water
¾ cup sugar
¼ teaspoon salt
16 ounces bittersweet chocolate
　(about 2⅔ cups chips or pieces)
1 cup salted butter (2 sticks)
6 large eggs
1 teaspoon GF pure vanilla extract

Poured Chocolate Ganache (recipe
　follows)
2 cups fresh berries

TO MAKE THE CUPCAKES:

1. Preheat the oven to 300°F. Brush the cupcake tins with the melted butter.
2. In a medium saucepan, stir together the water, sugar, and salt.
3. Add the chocolate and butter and heat over medium-low heat, stirring until the chocolate and butter are completely melted.
4. In a large bowl, whisk together the eggs and vanilla.
5. Slowly pour the chocolate mixture into the egg mixture, whisking constantly.
6. Divide the batter evenly among the prepared cups. Each cup should be filled almost to the top.
7. Bake for 30 minutes.
8. Allow the cupcakes to cool in the tins for 10 minutes.
9. Carefully run the tip of a thin knife around each cupcake to separate the cake from the edges of the tins. Turn the tins over onto a wire rack so the cupcakes drop out. Let them cool completely.
10. While the cupcakes are cooling, make the Poured Chocolate Ganache.

11. Place a sheet pan or cookie sheet beneath your cooling rack to catch any excess ganache.

12. Pour the ganache over each cupcake and use a knife to spread it toward the edges, allowing it to run down the sides.

13. Garnish with the fresh berries.

14. Serve the cupcakes with plates and forks.

POURED CHOCOLATE GANACHE

12 ounces bittersweet chocolate (about 2 cups chips or pieces)
1½ cups heavy cream

1. Put the chocolate in a bowl.
2. Heat the heavy cream to a simmer in a saucepan.
3. Pour the cream over the chocolate and let sit for 1 minute.
4. Stir the chocolate and cream together until the chocolate melts completely. Use the ganache while it is still warm.

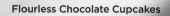
Flourless Chocolate Cupcakes

German Chocolate Cupcake

german chocolate cupcakes

MAKES 24 CUPCAKES

Contrary to popular belief, German chocolate cake didn't originate in Germany. It was named for Sam German, who developed a sweet version of baking chocolate for the Baker's Chocolate Company in the 1850s. Traditionally, German chocolate cake is a layered chocolate cake with coconut pecan frosting between the layers and on top of the cake. For Kelli, the cake is merely a delivery mechanism for the frosting, but for Pete, it's the total package that truly delivers. Our recipe calls for semi-sweet chocolate, which we've found is more widely available in supermarkets than German sweet chocolate. The semi-sweet chocolate has slightly more cacao and slightly less sugar, but it works exceptionally well in this recipe. Mr. German would be proud.

¼ cup very hot water

5 ounces semi-sweet chocolate
   (chips or pieces) (about ¾ cup)

1 cup salted butter (2 sticks), room
   temperature

2 cups sugar

1 teaspoon GF pure vanilla extract

4 large eggs, room temperature

1 cup buttermilk, room temperature

3 cups Artisan Gluten-Free Flour
   Blend (page 10)

2 teaspoons xanthan gum

1½ teaspoons GF baking powder

1½ teaspoons GF baking soda

½ teaspoon salt

Coconut Pecan Frosting (recipe follows)

TO MAKE THE CUPCAKES:

1. Preheat the oven to 350°F. Line standard cupcake tins with paper liners.

2. Place the hot water and chocolate together in a small bowl, and let stand 1 minute. Stir until the chocolate is completely melted. Set aside.

3. With an electric mixer, cream together the butter and sugar until light and fluffy, then add the vanilla.

4. Add the eggs one at a time, mixing to incorporate after each addition.

5. Add the buttermilk and chocolate mixture (from step 2), and mix until combined.

6. In a separate bowl, combine the flour, xanthan gum, baking powder, baking soda, and salt, and mix with a whisk

to "sift" the ingredients and break up any lumps.

7. Add the dry ingredients all at once to the sugar mixture and mix for about 10 seconds at medium-low speed to incorporate.

8. Scrape down the sides of the bowl and mix at high speed for about 5 seconds, just until the batter is completely mixed and smooth.

9. Divide the batter evenly among the paper-lined cups. Make the top of the batter as smooth as you can.

10. Bake for 25 minutes.

11. Allow the cupcakes to cool in the tins for 10 minutes, then remove from the tins and let cool completely on a wire rack.

12. While the cupcakes are cooling, make the Coconut Pecan Frosting.

TO FINISH THE CUPCAKES:

13. Remove the paper liners and slice each cupcake in half horizontally with a serrated knife.

14. Spread 1 tablespoon of the Coconut Pecan Frosting on the bottom half of each cupcake, and place the top half on the spread frosting.

15. Spread 1 heaping tablespoon of the frosting on top of each cupcake.

COCONUT PECAN FROSTING

2½ cups chopped pecans
2 cups packed brown sugar
2 cups evaporated milk
1 cup salted butter (2 sticks)
6 large egg yolks
3 cups sweetened coconut flakes
2 teaspoons GF pure vanilla extract
½ teaspoon salt

1. In the 350°F preheated oven, toast the pecans in a single layer on a cookie sheet for about 10 minutes, until the nuts are fragrant. (Be careful not to burn the pecans, which will turn them bitter.)
2. In a heavy saucepan, heat the brown sugar, evaporated milk, butter, and egg yolks over medium heat, stirring occasionally, for about 12 minutes, until thick and bubbly.
3. Remove from the heat, add the pecans, coconut, vanilla, and salt, and stir to mix. Allow the frosting to cool completely before frosting the cupcakes.

Mocha Cupcake

mocha cupcakes

MAKES 24 CUPCAKES

Our mocha cupcake is unabashedly inspired by the beloved café mocha, a drink usually made with a combination of espresso and chocolate (sweetened cocoa powder, chocolate syrup, or melted chocolate). In cupcake form, the chocolate of the cake perfectly balances against the coffee of the buttercream. Our secret is the use of instant coffee, made by freeze- or spray-drying brewed coffee, a process that removes the water from the coffee, leaving behind dried coffee crystals with intense flavor.

1 cup salted butter (2 sticks)

1 cup water

½ cup unsweetened cocoa powder (regular or dark)

5 tablespoons instant coffee

2 cups sugar

2 large eggs

1 cup sour cream

2 tablespoons coffee-flavored liqueur

2½ cups Artisan Gluten-Free Flour Blend (page 10)

2 teaspoons xanthan gum

1½ teaspoons GF baking powder

1½ teaspoons GF baking soda

½ teaspoon salt

Mocha Buttercream (recipe follows)

Unsweetened cocoa powder

TO MAKE THE CUPCAKES:

1. Preheat the oven to 350°F. Line standard cupcake tins with paper liners.

2. Heat the butter, water, cocoa, and instant coffee over medium heat in a saucepan until the butter is melted.

3. Meanwhile, put the sugar in a mixing bowl. Add the butter-cocoa mixture and mix at low speed for about 5 minutes, or until the mixture is cool.

4. Add the eggs one at a time, mixing to incorporate after each addition.

5. Add the sour cream and liqueur, mix to incorporate, and scrape down the sides of the bowl.

6. In a separate bowl, combine the flour, xanthan gum, baking powder, baking soda, and salt, and mix with a whisk to "sift" the ingredients and break up any lumps.

7. Add the dry ingredients to the cocoa–sour cream mixture and mix for about 10 seconds at medium-low speed to incorporate.

8. Scrape down the sides thoroughly and mix for an additional 5 seconds at high speed, just until everything is mixed and smooth.

9. Divide the batter evenly among the paper-lined cups. Make the top of the batter as smooth as you can.

10. Bake for 25 minutes.

11. Allow the cupcakes to cool in the tins for 10 minutes, then remove from the tins and let cool completely on a wire rack.

12. While the cupcakes are cooling, make the Mocha Buttercream.

TO FINISH THE CUPCAKES:

13. Use a large open tip to pipe small dollops of Mocha Buttercream on the cupcakes, starting at the edge and working toward the center.

14. Add a second and third tier to give it height.

15. Using a fine metal mesh sieve, dust the cupcakes with the cocoa powder.

MOCHA BUTTERCREAM

1⅓ cups plus 1 tablespoon sugar, divided
½ cup plus 1 tablespoon water, divided
4 large egg whites
¼ teaspoon salt
1½ cups salted butter (3 sticks), removed from the refrigerator when you start the buttercream
8 ounces semi-sweet chocolate, melted and cooled
1 tablespoon instant coffee

1. Mix 1⅓ cups of the sugar and ½ cup of the water in a heavy saucepan. Put a candy thermometer in the sugar mixture and heat to 240°F without stirring.
2. Meanwhile, in a stand mixer using the whisk attachment, whisk the egg whites and salt at medium-high speed until frothy.
3. Add the remaining 1 tablespoon of sugar to the egg whites and whisk until soft peaks form. Turn the mixer off and let the egg whites sit until the sugar comes up to temperature.
4. When the sugar mixture reaches 240°F, with the mixer at medium speed, slowly drizzle the hot sugar mixture down the side of the bowl into the beaten egg whites.
5. After all the sugar is added, continue whisking the mixture until it is cool, about 10 minutes.
6. While the egg whites are whisking, cut the butter into tablespoon-size pieces.
7. When the egg whites are cool, leave the mixer running at medium speed and add the butter, 1 tablespoon at a time, allowing enough time for each tablespoon of butter to incorporate after each addition, until all the butter is added.

continued

8. Add the chocolate and mix to combine.
9. Dissolve the instant coffee in the remaining 1 tablespoon of water.
10. Switch to the paddle attachment, add the coffee, and mix for an additional 1 to 2 minutes at medium-high speed until the air bubbles are out of the frosting and the frosting is silky smooth.

sweet surprises

Who doesn't love a sweet surprise? These filled cupcakes contain hidden treasure, whether Strawberry Jelly Donut Filling, Cinnamon Apple Pie Filling, Key Lime Filling, or sweet Pastry Cream. Don't judge these books by the cover. The first bite reveals their true character.

Fruit Tart Cupcakes

fruit tart cupcakes

MAKES 24 CUPCAKES

Fruit tarts follow a simple formula: Start with a sweet pastry dough crust, add a rich and smooth pastry cream filling, top it with colorful fresh fruit, and brush it with a glaze to impart the signature shine. We didn't see any reason this time-tested combination couldn't be reborn as a cupcake. In fact, this recipe is like eating a genuine mini fruit tart—there's the Pastry Cream, the fruit, and the glaze, with a cupcake as the stand-in for the pastry dough crust.

¾ cup salted butter (1½ sticks), room
    temperature
1¾ cups sugar
2 teaspoons GF pure vanilla extract
2 large eggs, room temperature
2 large egg whites, room temperature
1 cup milk
¼ cup sour cream
3 cups Artisan Gluten-Free Flour
    Blend (page 10)
2 teaspoons xanthan gum
2½ teaspoons GF baking powder
1 teaspoon GF baking soda
½ teaspoon salt

Pastry Cream (recipe follows)
Fruit (strawberries, blueberries,
    raspberries, kiwi, mandarin
    oranges, etc.)
Apple Glaze (recipe follows) (see
    Note, next page)

TO MAKE THE CUPCAKES:

1. Preheat the oven to 350°F. Line standard cupcake tins with paper liners.

2. With an electric mixer, cream together the butter and sugar until fluffy, then add the vanilla.

3. Add the eggs and egg whites one at a time, mixing to incorporate after each addition.

4. Add the milk and sour cream, and mix until combined.

5. In a separate bowl, combine the flour, xanthan gum, baking powder, baking soda, and salt, and mix with a whisk to "sift" the ingredients and break up any lumps.

6. Add the dry ingredients all at once to the sugar mixture and mix for about 10 seconds at medium-low speed to incorporate.

7. Scrape down the sides of the bowl and mix at high speed for about 5 seconds,

just until the batter is completely mixed and smooth.

8. Divide the batter evenly among the paper-lined cups. Make the top of the batter as smooth as you can.

9. Bake for 25 minutes.

10. Allow the cupcakes to cool in the tins for 10 minutes, then remove from the tins and let cool completely on a wire rack.

11. While the cupcakes are cooling, make the Pastry Cream and the Apple Glaze.

TO FINISH THE CUPCAKES:

12. When the cupcakes are cool, cut an inverted cone into the top of each cupcake that is about 2 inches in diameter and 1 inch deep. After the cone is removed, use the tip of your knife to hollow out the cupcake, removing additional crumbs until you have a hole with straight sides. Take care not to break through the bottom of your cupcake. Discard or compost the cupcake tops (or nibble on them while you're making the rest of the recipe!). (For detailed step-by-step instructions with photos, see page 27.)

13. Fill each cupcake with 1 heaping table-spoon of cooled Pastry Cream, using enough to bring it level with the top of the cupcake.

14. Decorate the top of the cream with fresh fruit.

15. Use a pastry brush to brush the cooled Apple Glaze on the fruit to make all the fruit shiny.

PASTRY CREAM

½ **cup sugar**
¼ **cup cornstarch**
4 large egg yolks
2 cups milk
1 tablespoon plus 1 teaspoon salted butter
2 teaspoons GF pure vanilla extract

1. Mix the sugar and cornstarch in a small bowl.
2. Whisk in the egg yolks, beating until light in color. (The sugar-cornstarch–egg yolk mixture will be very thick, but don't give up! As you beat it, it *will* become pale yellow.)
3. Heat the milk in a small saucepan over high heat to bring to a boil, then remove from the heat.
4. Temper the egg yolk mixture by slowly pouring about half the hot milk into it while vigorously whisking. Continuing to whisk, pour the tempered eggs back into the remaining milk in the saucepan and return to the heat.
5. Bring the mixture to a boil and cook, whisking constantly, for 1 minute.
6. Remove from the heat and stir in the butter and vanilla.
7. Immediately transfer the Pastry Cream to a container and place a piece of plastic wrap directly on the surface of the cream. (This prevents a skin from forming.)
8. Refrigerate until cool. Whisk until smooth just before using.

APPLE GLAZE

½ cup apple juice
1 teaspoon cornstarch

1. Mix the apple juice and cornstarch in a small saucepan.
2. Cook over medium-high heat, stirring constantly, until the mixture comes to a boil, turns clear, and thickens.
3. Remove from the heat and let cool to room temperature.

Note: For a quick and easy shortcut, you can use jarred apple or apricot jelly in lieu of making a from-scratch glaze. Simply melt a small amount of jelly by heating (in a small pot or in the microwave) and use it as your glaze. You can also add a small amount of water if the glaze is too thick.

key lime pie cupcakes

MAKES 24 CUPCAKES

Originating in Key West, Florida, key lime pie is made with the tiny, tart key limes found in that region (compared to the larger, sweeter Persian lime). The filling for which the pie is known is made with lime juice, sweetened condensed milk, and often eggs, though our version uses mascarpone cheese. With the cupcake, the key lime filling, the whipped cream, and a bit of lime zest to garnish, the result is a well-balanced cupcake with a limey, light and refreshing flavor.

¾ cup salted butter (1½ sticks), room temperature

1¾ cups sugar

2 teaspoons GF pure vanilla extract

2 large eggs, room temperature

2 large egg whites, room temperature

1 cup milk

¼ cup sour cream

3 cups Artisan Gluten-Free Flour Blend (page 10)

2 teaspoons xanthan gum

2½ teaspoons GF baking powder

1 teaspoon GF baking soda

½ teaspoon salt

Key Lime Filling (recipe follows)
Whipped Cream (recipe follows)
Zest of 2 limes

TO MAKE THE CUPCAKES:

1. Preheat the oven to 350°F. Line standard cupcake tins with paper liners.

2. With an electric mixer, cream together the butter and sugar until fluffy, then add the vanilla.

3. Add the eggs and egg whites one at a time, mixing to incorporate after each addition.

4. Add the milk and sour cream, and mix until combined.

5. In a separate bowl, combine the flour, xanthan gum, baking powder, baking soda, and salt, and mix with a whisk to "sift" the ingredients and break up any lumps.

6. Add the dry ingredients all at once to the sugar mixture and mix for about 10 seconds at medium-low speed to incorporate.

7. Scrape down the sides of the bowl and mix at high speed for about 5 seconds, just until the batter is completely mixed and smooth.
8. Divide the batter evenly among the paper-lined cups. Make the top of the batter as smooth as you can.
9. Bake for 25 minutes.
10. Allow the cupcakes to cool in the tins for 10 minutes, then remove from the tins and let cool completely on a wire rack.
11. While the cupcakes are cooling, make the Key Lime Filling and the Whipped Cream.

TO FINISH THE CUPCAKES:

12. When the cupcakes are cool, cut an inverted cone into the top of each cupcake that is about 1½ inches in diameter and 1 inch deep. Cut off the point of the cone and save the top to serve as a lid for the hole in the cupcake. After the cone is removed, use the tip of your knife to hollow out the cupcake, removing additional crumbs until you have a hole with straight sides. Take care not to break through the bottom of your cupcake. (For detailed step-by-step instructions with photos, see page 27.)
13. Fill each cupcake with about 2 teaspoons of the Key Lime Filling and place the reserved cap on top of the filling, sealing the cupcake.
14. Use a small palette knife to spread the Whipped Cream on the cupcakes.
15. Garnish with the fresh lime zest.

KEY LIME FILLING

Zest of 4 key limes (or about 1 tablespoon or the zest of 1 Persian lime)
½ cup fresh lime juice (about 8 to 10 key limes or 2 to 3 Persian limes) (see Note)
One 14-ounce can sweetened condensed milk
⅓ cup mascarpone cheese

With an electric mixer or whisk, mix the zest, juice, condensed milk, and cheese.

Note: Be sure to zest the limes first before juicing. Zesting already-juiced limes is nearly impossible!

Key Lime Cupcakes

WHIPPED CREAM

2 cups heavy cream
2 tablespoons confectioners' sugar
2 teaspoons GF pure vanilla extract

1. Chill a metal mixing bowl and a whisk or eggbeaters in the freezer for 5 minutes.
2. Pour the cream into the cold bowl and whisk until it starts to thicken.
3. Add the confectioners' sugar and vanilla, and whisk until soft peaks form. Do not over-mix or the over-whipped cream will take on a curdled appearance. (If this does happen, it's purely a cosmetic issue and won't affect the taste of your whipped cream.)

jelly donut cupcakes

This is a cupcake with a sweet surprise in the center. Inspired by the Dunkin Donuts jelly donut (alas, not gluten-free), our Jelly Donut Cupcakes have a strawberry filling that tastes like a dead ringer (as best as our memory serves us from our gluten days years ago) for the DD version.

¾ cup salted butter (1½ sticks), room temperature

1¾ cups sugar

2 teaspoons GF pure vanilla extract

2 large eggs, room temperature

2 large egg whites, room temperature

1 cup milk

¼ cup sour cream

3 cups Artisan Gluten-Free Flour Blend (page 10)

2 teaspoons xanthan gum

2½ teaspoons GF baking powder

1 teaspoon GF baking soda

½ teaspoon salt

Strawberry Jelly Donut Filling (recipe follows)

Jelly Donut Buttercream (recipe follows)

TO MAKE THE CUPCAKES:

1. Preheat the oven to 350°F. Line standard cupcake tins with paper liners.
2. With an electric mixer, cream together the butter and sugar until fluffy, then add the vanilla.
3. Add the eggs and egg whites one at a time, mixing to incorporate after each addition.
4. Add the milk and sour cream and mix until combined.
5. In a separate bowl, combine the flour, xanthan gum, baking powder, baking soda, and salt, and mix with a whisk to "sift" the ingredients and break up any lumps.
6. Add the dry ingredients all at once to the sugar mixture and mix for about 10 seconds at medium-low speed to incorporate.
7. Scrape down the sides of the bowl and mix at high speed for about 5 seconds,

just until the batter is completely mixed and smooth.

8. Divide the batter evenly among the paper-lined cups. Make the top of the batter as smooth as you can.

9. Bake for 25 minutes.

10. Allow the cupcakes to cool in the tins for 10 minutes, then remove from the tins and let cool completely on a wire rack.

11. While the cupcakes are cooling, make the Strawberry Jelly Donut Filling and then the Jelly Donut Buttercream.

TO FINISH THE CUPCAKES:

12. When the cupcakes are cool, cut an inverted cone into the top of each cupcake that is about 1½ inches in diameter and 1 inch deep. Cut off the point of the cone and save the top to serve as a lid for the hole in the cupcake. After the cone is removed, use the tip of your knife to hollow out the cupcake, removing additional crumbs until you have a hole with straight sides. Take care not to break through the bottom of your cupcake. (For detailed step-by-step instructions with photos, see page 27.)

13. Fill each cupcake with about 2 teaspoons of the Strawberry Jelly Donut Filling and place the reserved cap on top of the filling, sealing the cupcake (see Note).

14. Use a small palette knife to spread the Jelly Donut Buttercream on the cupcakes.

Note: If desired, set some of the Strawberry Jelly Donut Filling aside until the cupcakes have been frosted, and decorate the top of each cupcake with a small dollop.

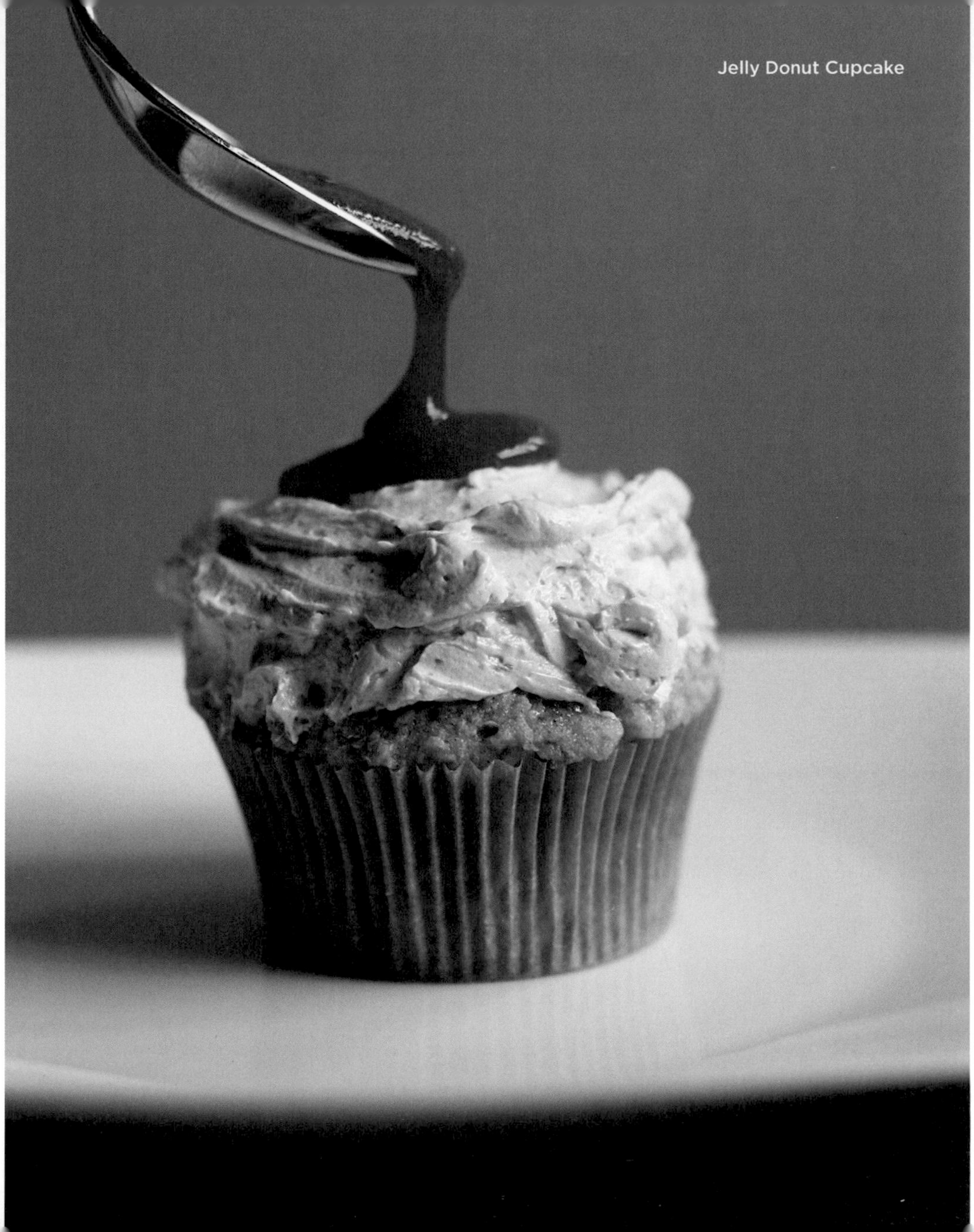

Jelly Donut Cupcake

STRAWBERRY JELLY DONUT FILLING

½ cup sugar
1 tablespoon cornstarch
3 tablespoons cool water
1 quart strawberries, sliced

1. Combine the sugar and cornstarch in a saucepan. Stir in the water. Add the strawberries and bring to a boil over medium-high heat, stirring constantly.
2. When the mixture comes to a boil, reduce the heat to medium and simmer until clear and thickened, about 4 minutes.
3. Remove from the heat and use an immersion blender or traditional blender to puree the filling until smooth. Cover and refrigerate until chilled.

Note: This filling can be made in advance and stored in the refrigerator up to 1 week until needed.

JELLY DONUT BUTTERCREAM

1⅓ cups plus 1 tablespoon sugar, divided

½ cup water

4 large egg whites

¼ teaspoon salt

1½ cups salted butter (3 sticks), removed from the refrigerator when you start the buttercream

2 teaspoons GF pure vanilla extract

¾ cup Strawberry Jelly Donut Filling (recipe on previous page), chilled

1. Mix 1⅓ cups of the sugar and the water in a heavy saucepan. Put a candy thermometer in the sugar mixture and heat to 240°F without stirring.
2. Meanwhile, in a stand mixer using a whisk attachment, whisk the egg whites and salt at medium-high speed until frothy.
3. Add the remaining 1 tablespoon of sugar to the egg whites and whisk until soft peaks form. Turn the mixer off and let the egg whites sit until the sugar comes up to temperature.
4. When the sugar mixture reaches 240°F, with the mixer at medium speed, slowly drizzle the hot sugar mixture down the side of the bowl into the beaten egg whites.
5. After all the sugar is added, continue whisking the mixture until it is cool, about 10 minutes.
6. While the egg whites are whisking, cut the butter into tablespoon-size pieces.
7. When the egg whites are cool, leave the mixer running at medium speed and add the butter, 1 tablespoon at a time, allowing enough time for each tablespoon of butter to incorporate after each addition, until all the butter is added.
8. Add the vanilla and mix to combine.
9. Switch to the paddle attachment and add the ¾ cup of Strawberry Jelly Donut Filling. Mix for an additional 1 or 2 minutes at medium-high speed until the air bubbles are out of the frosting and the frosting is silky smooth.

Boston Crème Cupcakes

boston crème cupcakes

MAKES 24 CUPCAKES

Born in its namesake city, a Boston cream pie is a cake filled with vanilla custard and topped with chocolate ganache. This cupcake doesn't fall far from the tree. If you're craving a gluten-free Boston cream pie, this recipe will deliver.

¾ cup salted butter (1½ sticks), room temperature

1¾ cups sugar

2 teaspoons GF pure vanilla extract

2 large eggs, room temperature

2 large egg whites, room temperature

1 cup milk

¼ cup sour cream

3 cups Artisan Gluten-Free Flour Blend (page 10)

2 teaspoons xanthan gum

2½ teaspoons GF baking powder

1 teaspoon GF baking soda

½ teaspoon salt

Pastry Cream (recipe follows)

Spread Chocolate Ganache (recipe follows)

TO MAKE THE CUPCAKES:

1. Preheat the oven to 350°F. Line standard cupcake tins with paper liners.

2. With an electric mixer, cream together the butter and sugar until fluffy, then add the vanilla.

3. Add the eggs and egg whites one at a time, mixing to incorporate after each addition. Add the milk and sour cream, and mix until combined.

4. In a separate bowl, combine the flour, xanthan gum, baking powder, baking soda, and salt, and mix with a whisk to "sift" the ingredients and break up any lumps.

5. Add the dry ingredients all at once to the sugar mixture and mix for about 10 seconds at medium-low speed to incorporate.

6. Scrape down the sides of the bowl and mix at high speed for about 5 seconds, just until the batter is completely mixed and smooth.

7. Divide the batter evenly among the paper-lined cups. Make the top of the batter as smooth as you can.

8. Bake for 25 minutes.
9. Allow the cupcakes to cool in the tins for 10 minutes, then remove from the tins and let cool completely on a wire rack.
10. While the cupcakes are cooling, make the Pastry Cream and the Spread Chocolate Ganache.

TO FINISH THE CUPCAKES:

11. When the cupcakes are cool, cut an inverted cone into the top of each cupcake that is about 1½ inches in diameter and 1 inch deep. Cut off the point of the cone and save the top to serve as a lid for the hole in the cupcake. After the cone is removed, use the tip of your knife to hollow out the cupcake, removing additional crumbs until you have a hole with straight sides. Take care not to break through the bottom of your cupcake. (For detailed step-by-step instructions with photos, see page 27.)
12. Fill each cupcake with about 2 teaspoons of Pastry Cream and place the reserved cap on top of the filling, sealing the cupcake.
13. Use a small palette knife to spread a smooth layer of Spread Chocolate Ganache on the cupcakes.

SPREAD CHOCOLATE GANACHE

8 ounces bittersweet chocolate (about 1⅓ cups chocolate chips or pieces)

¾ cup heavy cream

1. Put the chocolate in a bowl.
2. Heat the heavy cream to a simmer in a saucepan.
3. Pour the cream over the chocolate and let sit for 1 minute.
4. Stir the chocolate and cream together until the chocolate melts completely.
5. Let the ganache sit at room temperature until you use it. (If making more than 2 hours in advance, refrigerate and bring back to room temperature before use. This will result in a less shiny finished product.) It can be used slightly warm, but if it is too warm, it will run down the sides of the cupcake.

PASTRY CREAM

¼ cup plus 2 tablespoons sugar
3 tablespoons cornstarch
3 large egg yolks
1½ cups milk
1 tablespoon salted butter
1½ teaspoons GF pure vanilla extract

1. Mix together the sugar and cornstarch in a small bowl.
2. Whisk in the egg yolks, beating until light in color. (The sugar-cornstarch-egg yolk mixture will be very thick, but don't give up! As you beat it, it *will* become pale yellow.)
3. Heat the milk in a small saucepan over high heat to bring to a boil, then remove from the heat.
4. Temper the egg yolk mixture by slowly pouring about half the hot milk into the egg mixture while vigorously whisking. Pour the tempered eggs back into the remaining milk in the saucepan while whisking and return to the heat.
5. Bring the mixture to a boil and cook, whisking constantly, for 1 minute.
6. Remove from the heat and stir in the butter and vanilla.
7. Immediately transfer the Pastry Cream to a container and place a piece of plastic wrap directly on the surface of the cream. (This prevents a skin from forming.)
8. Refrigerate until cool. Whisk until smooth just before using.

Caramel Apple Pie Cupcakes

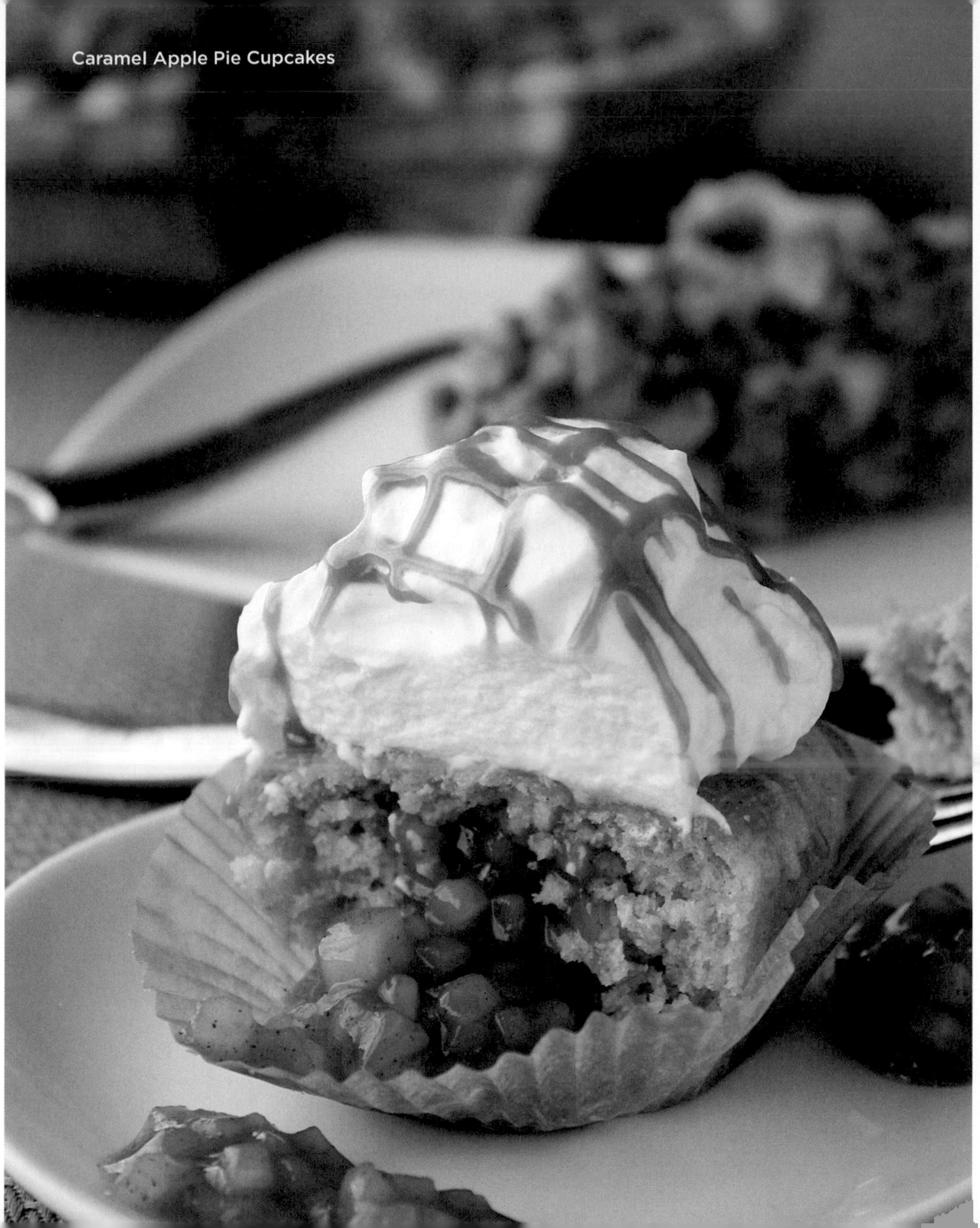

caramel apple pie cupcakes

MAKES 24 CUPCAKES

This recipe truly makes a fully realized apple pie reborn as a cupcake. Vanilla cake serves as the pie crust, which we fill with finely diced cinnamon apples. A traditional à la mode pie would be topped with ice cream, but we top these cupcakes with fresh whipped cream as a kind of faux la mode. To finish it off, we drizzle the cupcake with a basic Caramel Sauce. It is, in a word, divine.

¾ cup salted butter (1½ sticks), room temperature

1¾ cups sugar

2 teaspoons GF pure vanilla extract

4 large eggs, room temperature

1¼ cups buttermilk, room temperature

3 cups Artisan Gluten-Free Flour Blend (page 10)

2 teaspoons xanthan gum

2½ teaspoons GF baking powder

1 teaspoon GF baking soda

½ teaspoon salt

Cinnamon Apple Pie Filling (recipe follows)

Whipped Cream (recipe follows)

Caramel Sauce (recipe follows)

TO MAKE THE CUPCAKES:

1. Preheat the oven to 350°F. Line standard cupcake tins with paper liners.

2. With an electric mixer, cream together the butter and sugar until light and fluffy, then add the vanilla.

3. Add the eggs one at a time, mixing to incorporate after each addition.

4. Add the buttermilk and mix until combined.

5. In a separate bowl, combine the flour, xanthan gum, baking powder, baking soda, and salt, and mix with a whisk to "sift" the ingredients and break up any lumps.

6. Add the dry ingredients all at once to the sugar mixture and mix for about 10 seconds at medium-low speed to incorporate.

7. Scrape down the sides of the bowl and mix at high speed for about 5 seconds, just until the batter is completely mixed and smooth.

8. Divide the batter evenly among the paper-lined cups. Make the top of the batter as smooth as you can.

9. Bake for 25 minutes.
10. Allow the cupcakes to cool in the tins for 10 minutes, then remove from the tins and let cool completely on a wire rack.
11. While the cupcakes are cooling, make the Cinnamon Apple Pie Filling, the Caramel Sauce, and the Whipped Cream.

TO FINISH THE CUPCAKES:

12. When the cupcakes are cool, cut an inverted cone into the top of each cupcake that is about 1½ inches in diameter and 1 inch deep. Cut off the point of the cone and save the top to serve as a lid for the hole in the cupcake. After the cone is removed, use the tip of your knife to hollow out the cupcake, removing additional crumbs until you have a hole with straight sides. Take care not to break through the bottom of your cupcake. (For detailed step-by-step instructions with photos, see page 27.)

13. Fill each cupcake with 1 heaping tablespoon of the Cinnamon Apple Pie Filling and place the reserved top on the filling, sealing the cupcake.
14. Place a dollop of Whipped Cream on top of each cupcake.
15. Drizzle with the Caramel Sauce.

WHIPPED CREAM

2 cups heavy cream
2 tablespoons confectioners' sugar
2 teaspoons GF pure vanilla extract

1. Chill a metal mixing bowl and a whisk or eggbeaters in the freezer for 5 minutes.
2. Pour the cream into the cold bowl and whisk until it starts to thicken.
3. Add the confectioners' sugar and vanilla, and whisk until soft peaks form. Do not over-mix or the over-whipped cream will take on a curdled appearance. (If this does happen, it's purely a cosmetic issue and won't affect the taste of your whipped cream.)

CINNAMON APPLE PIE FILLING

1 tablespoon cornstarch
3 tablespoons sugar
1 teaspoon ground cinnamon
1 cup cool water
1½ cups apple, peeled, cored, and finely diced
1 teaspoon lemon juice

1. In a small saucepan, combine the cornstarch, sugar, and cinnamon. Add the water and stir to mix.
2. Add the apples, stir or toss to coat, and cook over medium-high heat to bring the mixture to a simmer.
3. Simmer for 5 minutes, until the mixture is thick and clear.
4. Remove from the heat, add the lemon juice, and stir. Set aside to cool to room temperature.

CARAMEL SAUCE

¾ cup sugar
3 tablespoons water
¾ cup heavy cream
½ teaspoon GF pure vanilla extract

1. In a medium saucepan, stir together the sugar and water. Place over high heat and let the sugar mixture cook without stirring until golden brown. (If the sugar starts to brown in just one area, gently swirl the pan; it will agitate the mixture just enough to distribute the heat. Do not stir.) If the sugar is pale yellow, it needs to cook a little longer; if it is dark brown, it has cooked too long.

2. As soon as the mixture is golden brown, carefully add the cream all at once and pull your hand back. (The heat of the sugar will instantly boil some of the cream, which might spatter for a few seconds.) Stir vigorously and cook for about 2 minutes, until the sugar and cream melt together and create a beautiful, smooth texture.

3. Remove from the heat, add the vanilla, stir, and let cool.

napoleon cupcakes

Also known as a mille-feuille ("thousand leaves"), a napoleon is a French dessert consisting of layers of puff pastry alternating with layers of pastry cream, topped with white icing or glaze and chocolate strips that are "combed" to create the dessert's signature look. It looks elegant and complicated but is actually quite easy to do. Here a cupcake serves as the puff pastry, but otherwise, all traditional napoleon elements are present.

¾ cup salted butter (1½ sticks), room temperature

1¾ cups sugar

2 teaspoons GF pure vanilla extract

2 large eggs, room temperature

2 large egg whites, room temperature

1 cup milk

¼ cup sour cream

3 cups Artisan Gluten-Free Flour Blend (page 10)

2 teaspoons xanthan gum

2½ teaspoons GF baking powder

1 teaspoon GF baking soda

½ teaspoon salt

Pastry Cream (recipe follows)

½ cup bittersweet chocolate chips or pieces

Napoleon Glaze (recipe follows)

TO MAKE THE CUPCAKES:

1. Preheat the oven to 350°F. Line standard cupcake tins with paper liners.

2. With an electric mixer, cream together the butter and sugar until fluffy, then add the vanilla.

3. Add the eggs and egg whites one at a time, mixing to incorporate after each addition.

4. Add the milk and sour cream, and mix until combined.

5. In a separate bowl, combine the flour, xanthan gum, baking powder, baking soda, and salt, and mix with a whisk to "sift" the ingredients and break up any lumps.

6. Add the dry ingredients all at once to the sugar mixture and mix for about 10 seconds at medium-low speed to incorporate.

7. Scrape down the sides of the bowl and mix at high speed for about 5 seconds, just until the batter is completely mixed and smooth.

8. Divide the batter evenly among the paper-lined cups. Make the top of the batter as smooth as you can.

9. Bake for 25 minutes.

10. Allow the cupcakes to cool in the tins for 10 minutes, then remove from the tins and let cool completely on a wire rack.

11. While the cupcakes are cooling, make the Pastry Cream and the Napoleon Glaze.

TO FINISH THE CUPCAKES:

12. When the cupcakes are cool, use a serrated knife to "shave" the top of the cupcake, making a perfectly flat top. Then cut an inverted cone into the top of each cupcake that is about 1½ inches in diameter and 1 inch deep. Cut off the point of the cone and save the top to serve as a lid for the hole in the cupcake. After the cone is removed, use the tip of your knife to hollow out the cupcake, removing additional crumbs until you have a hole with straight sides. Take care not to break through the bottom of your cupcake. (For detailed step-by-step instructions with photos, see page 27.)

13. Fill each cupcake with about 2 teaspoons of Pastry Cream and place the reserved cap on top of the filling, sealing the cupcake.

14. In a separate bowl, melt the bittersweet chocolate. Let the chocolate cool to room temperature before using.

15. Put the chocolate into a zip-top bag or pastry bag and cut a very small hole in the corner, large enough to squeeze out a thin bead of chocolate.

16. Carefully spread a thin layer of the Napoleon Glaze on top of the cupcake. Using the prepared bag with the melted chocolate, make a series of thin parallel lines of chocolate across the top of the glaze.

17. Drag the tip of a toothpick through the chocolate and glaze several times, perpendicular to the direction of the thin chocolate lines. Alternate the direction of the "drags" each time (first left to right, then right to left, etc.)—this creates the traditional squiggle pattern of a napoleon.

Napoleon Cupcake

PASTRY CREAM

¼ cup plus 2 tablespoons sugar
3 tablespoons cornstarch
3 large egg yolks
1½ cups milk
1 tablespoon salted butter
1½ teaspoons GF pure vanilla extract

1. Mix together the sugar and cornstarch in a small bowl.
2. Whisk in the egg yolks, beating until light in color. (The sugar-cornstarch–egg yolk mixture will be very thick, but don't give up! As you beat it, it *will* become pale yellow.)
3. Heat the milk in a small saucepan over high heat to bring to a boil, then remove from the heat.
4. Temper the egg yolk mixture by slowly pouring about half the hot milk into the egg mixture while vigorously whisking. Pour the tempered eggs back into the remaining milk in the saucepan while whisking, and return to the heat.
5. Bring the mixture to a boil and cook, whisking constantly, for 1 minute.
6. Remove from the heat and stir in the butter and vanilla.
7. Immediately transfer the Pastry Cream to a container and place a piece of plastic wrap directly on the surface of the cream. (This prevents a skin from forming.)
8. Refrigerate until cool. Whisk until smooth just before using.

NAPOLEON GLAZE

2¼ cups confectioners' sugar
3 tablespoons milk

Mix the confectioners' sugar and milk until the sugar is fully dissolved in the milk and the icing is smooth.

old faithfuls

These nostalgic cupcakes are throwbacks to the desserts of yesteryear—an ice cream sundae, an orange creamsicle pop, a rum raisin cake. Their familiar flavor combinations will be a trip down memory lane.

Banana Split Cupcakes

banana split cupcakes

MAKES 24 CUPCAKES

Dating to the early 1900s, a classic banana split includes three flavors of ice cream—vanilla, chocolate, and strawberry—plus whipped cream and, of course, bananas. We re-imagine the banana split in this cupcake, pairing a vanilla cupcake with whipped cream that's drizzled with chocolate and strawberry sauces and, finally, topped off with several slices of banana.

¾ cup salted butter (1½ sticks), room temperature

1¾ cups sugar

2 teaspoons GF pure vanilla extract

2 large eggs, room temperature

2 large egg whites, room temperature

1 cup milk

¼ cup sour cream

3 cups Artisan Gluten-Free Flour Blend (page 10)

2 teaspoons xanthan gum

2½ teaspoons GF baking powder

1 teaspoon GF baking soda

½ teaspoon salt

Whipped Cream (recipe follows)

Chocolate Sauce (recipe follows)

Strawberry Sauce (recipe follows)

2 bananas, peeled and sliced into thin coins

TO MAKE THE CUPCAKES:

1. Preheat the oven to 350°F. Line standard cupcake tins with paper liners.

2. With an electric mixer, cream together the butter and sugar until fluffy, then add the vanilla.

3. Add the eggs and egg whites one at a time, mixing to incorporate after each addition.

4. Add the milk and sour cream and mix until combined.

5. In a separate bowl, combine the flour, xanthan gum, baking powder, baking soda, and salt, and mix with a whisk to "sift" the ingredients and break up any lumps.

6. Add the dry ingredients all at once to the sugar mixture and mix for about 10 seconds at medium-low speed to incorporate.

7. Scrape down the sides of the bowl and mix at high speed for about 5 seconds,

just until the batter is completely mixed and smooth.

8. Divide the batter evenly among the paper-lined cups. Make the top of the batter as smooth as you can.

9. Bake for 25 minutes.

10. Allow the cupcakes to cool in the tins for 10 minutes, then remove from the tins and let cool completely on a wire rack.

11. While the cupcakes are cooling, make the Chocolate Sauce, Strawberry Sauce, and Whipped Cream.

TO FINISH THE CUPCAKES:

12. Use a large star tip to pipe a spiral of Whipped Cream on the cupcakes.

13. Drizzle with the Chocolate Sauce and Strawberry Sauce.

14. Garnish each cupcake with four slices of banana.

WHIPPED CREAM

2 cups heavy cream
2 tablespoons confectioners' sugar
2 teaspoons GF pure vanilla extract

1. Chill a metal mixing bowl and a whisk or eggbeaters in the freezer for 5 minutes.

2. Pour the cream into the cold bowl and whisk until it starts to thicken.

3. Add the confectioners' sugar and vanilla, and whisk until soft peaks form. Do not over-mix or the over-whipped cream will take on a curdled appearance. (If this does happen, it's purely a cosmetic issue and won't affect the taste of your whipped cream.)

CHOCOLATE SAUCE

⅓ cup sugar
3 tablespoons unsweetened cocoa powder
⅓ cup corn syrup
⅓ cup evaporated milk
2 tablespoons salted butter
¼ teaspoon GF pure vanilla extract
Pinch salt (about ⅛ teaspoon)

1. Whisk together the sugar and cocoa in a medium saucepan.
2. Add the corn syrup, evaporated milk, butter, vanilla, and salt.
3. Cook over medium heat, stirring constantly.
4. Bring the mixture to a full boil and cook, stirring, for 5 minutes or until thick and glossy.
5. Remove the sauce from the heat and let cool to room temperature.

STRAWBERRY SAUCE

¼ cup sugar
1½ teaspoons cornstarch
2 tablespoons cool water
1 pint strawberries

1. Combine the sugar and cornstarch in a saucepan. Stir in the water. Add the strawberries and bring to a boil over medium-high heat, stirring constantly.
2. When the mixture comes to a boil, decrease the heat to medium and simmer until clear and thickened, about 4 minutes.
3. Remove from the heat and use an immersion blender or traditional blender to puree the filling until smooth. Let the sauce cool to room temperature.

Note: The Chocolate Sauce can be made in advance and stored in the refrigerator in a tightly covered container for up to 1 month. The same goes for the Strawberry Sauce, which can be stored for up to 1 week. Gently heat the sauces (separately, of course) in the microwave or on the stovetop to bring them back to pouring consistency.

Crumb Cake Cupcakes

crumb cake cupcakes

This cupcake is modeled after the New York–style crumb cakes Pete knew well as a child growing up on Long Island. It is a moist cake with a crumb top, finished off with a generous dose of confectioners' sugar. For the crumb topping, we go with a traditional German streusel. In lieu of a dusting of confectioners' sugar, we instead use a Confectioners' Sugar Icing to similar effect.

¾ cup salted butter (1½ sticks), room temperature

1¾ cups sugar

2 teaspoons GF pure vanilla extract

2 large eggs, room temperature

2 large egg whites, room temperature

1 cup milk

¼ cup sour cream

3 cups Artisan Gluten-Free Flour Blend (page 10)

2 teaspoons xanthan gum

2½ teaspoons GF baking powder

1 teaspoon GF baking soda

½ teaspoon salt

Streusel Topping (recipe follows)
Confectioners' Sugar Icing (recipe follows)

1. First, make the Streusel Topping.

TO MAKE THE CUPCAKES:

2. Preheat the oven to 350°F. Line standard cupcake tins with paper liners.

3. With an electric mixer, cream together the butter and sugar until fluffy, then add the vanilla.

4. Add the eggs and egg whites one at a time, mixing to incorporate after each addition.

5. Add the milk and sour cream, and mix until combined.

6. In a separate bowl, combine the flour, xanthan gum, baking powder, baking soda, and salt, and mix with a whisk to "sift" the ingredients and break up any lumps.

7. Add the dry ingredients all at once to the sugar mixture and mix for about 10 seconds at medium-low speed to incorporate.

8. Scrape down the sides of the bowl and mix at high speed for about 5 seconds, just until the batter is completely mixed and smooth.

9. Divide the batter evenly among the paper-lined cups. Make the top of the batter as smooth as you can.

10. Sprinkle the Streusel Topping on the cupcakes.

11. Bake for 25 minutes.

12. Allow the cupcakes to cool in the tins for 10 minutes, then remove from the tins and let cool completely on a wire rack.

13. When the cupcakes are nearly cool, make the Confectioners' Sugar Icing.

TO FINISH THE CUPCAKES:

14. Use a spoon to drizzle the Confectioners' Sugar Icing across the tops of the cupcakes.

STREUSEL TOPPING

1½ cups Artisan Gluten-Free Flour Blend (page 10)
¾ cup packed brown sugar
2 teaspoons ground cinnamon
¾ cup cold salted butter (1½ sticks butter), cut into small cubes

1. Mix the flour, brown sugar, and cinnamon together.
2. With your hands or a pastry cutter, mix in the butter until pea-size crumbles form.

CONFECTIONERS' SUGAR ICING

1 cup confectioners' sugar
2 tablespoons milk

Mix together the confectioners' sugar and milk until the sugar is fully dissolved in the milk and the icing is smooth.

gingerbread cupcakes

MAKES 24 CUPCAKES

Although it could be made year-round, to us this gingerbread cupcake evokes the holiday season. Featuring a spiced gingerbread cake topped with fresh whipped cream and garnished with Mini Gingerbread Girl and Boy Cookies, these cupcakes are fun and whimsical, and—when presented en masse on a tiered cupcake display—would make the perfect centerpiece for any holiday party. When making this recipe, allow extra time to bake a batch of the mini gluten-free gingerbread cookies first, or make them ahead of time so you're ready to go.

½ cup salted butter (1 stick), room temperature

½ cup packed brown sugar

2 large eggs

1 cup molasses

1 cup hot water

2½ cups Artisan Gluten-Free Flour Blend (page 10)

2 teaspoons xanthan gum

1½ teaspoons GF baking powder

1½ teaspoons GF baking soda

2 teaspoons ground cinnamon

2 teaspoons ground ginger

1 teaspoon ground cloves

¼ teaspoon salt

Whipped Cream (recipe follows)
Mini Gingerbread Girl and Boy
   Cookies (recipe follows)

1. First, make the Mini Gingerbread Girl and Boy Cookies.

TO MAKE THE CUPCAKES:

2. Preheat the oven to 350°F. Line standard cupcake tins with paper liners.

3. With an electric mixer, cream together the butter and sugar until light and fluffy.

4. Add the eggs one at a time, mixing to incorporate after each addition.

5. Add the molasses and hot water, mixing just to combine.

6. In a separate bowl, combine the flour, xanthan gum, baking powder, baking soda, cinnamon, ginger, cloves, and salt, and mix with a whisk to "sift" the ingredients and break up any lumps.

7. Add the dry ingredients all at once to the sugar mixture and mix for about

10 seconds at medium-low speed to incorporate.

8. Scrape down the sides of the bowl and mix at high speed for about 5 seconds, just until the batter is completely mixed and smooth.

9. Divide the batter evenly among the paper-lined cups. Make the top of the batter as smooth as you can.

10. Bake for 25 minutes.

11. Allow the cupcakes to cool in the tins for 10 minutes, then remove from the tins and let cool completely on a wire rack.

TO FINISH THE CUPCAKES:

12. Place a heavy dollop of Whipped Cream on each cupcake.

13. Garnish with a Mini Gingerbread Girl or Boy Cookie.

WHIPPED CREAM

2 cups heavy cream
2 tablespoons confectioners' sugar
2 teaspoons GF pure vanilla extract

1. Chill a metal mixing bowl and a whisk or eggbeaters in the freezer for 5 minutes.

2. Pour the cream into the cold bowl and whisk until it starts to thicken.

3. Add the confectioners' sugar and vanilla, and whisk until soft peaks form. Do not over-mix or the over-whipped cream will take on a curdled appearance. (If this does happen, it's purely a cosmetic issue and won't affect the taste of your whipped cream.)

Gingerbread Cupcakes

MINI GINGERBREAD GIRL AND BOY COOKIES

MAKES ABOUT 50 MINI COOKIES

¼ cup packed brown sugar
6 tablespoons salted butter (¾ stick), room temperature
⅓ cup molasses
½ teaspoon GF pure vanilla extract
1 large egg
1½ cups plus 2 tablespoons Artisan Gluten-Free Flour Blend (page 10)
1½ teaspoons xanthan gum
½ teaspoon GF baking soda
1 teaspoon ground cinnamon
1 teaspoon ground ginger
½ teaspoon ground allspice
½ teaspoon ground cloves
¼ teaspoon salt
Large round white GF sprinkles, optional

1. Preheat the oven to 375°F.
2. Cream together the brown sugar and the butter in an electric mixer until light and fluffy, then add the molasses and vanilla extract.
3. Stir in the egg, mixing to incorporate.
4. Stir in the flour, xanthan gum, baking soda, cinnamon, ginger, allspice, cloves, and salt.
5. Divide the dough, wrap each half in plastic wrap, and refrigerate for 30 minutes.
6. Remove one piece of dough from the plastic wrap and roll it out between two pieces of plastic wrap to a thickness of ¼ inch.
7. Remove the top piece of plastic wrap and, leaving the cookies in place, use a small cookie cutter to cut out the desired shapes in the entire sheet of dough.
8. Return the top piece of plastic wrap to the cookies and place them in the freezer for about 5 minutes, which will make removing the cookies from the surrounding dough much easier.
9. Remove the cookies from the freezer and transfer to an ungreased cookie sheet, placing them about ½ inch apart.
10. Repeat steps 6 to 9 with the second piece of dough.
11. If desired, decorate each gingerbread cookie with sprinkles for buttons.
12. Bake for 5 to 6 minutes, until slightly brown and set at the edges and the cookies are firm but still chewy.
13. Let the cookies rest on the cookie sheet for 2 minutes, then cool on a wire rack.

pumpkin spice cupcakes

MAKES 24 CUPCAKES

This cupcake is reminiscent of pumpkin pie topped with whipped cream. The spice from cinnamon, nutmeg, ginger, and cloves coupled with the pumpkin and a Cinnamon Whipped Cream make this cupcake stand out, especially during the fall season.

½ cup salted butter (2 sticks), room temperature

1¼ cups packed brown sugar

1 teaspoon GF pure vanilla extract

4 large eggs, room temperature

1²/₃ cups cooked pumpkin (or one 15-ounce can)

½ cup buttermilk, room temperature

2¾ cups Artisan Gluten-Free Flour Blend (page 10)

1½ teaspoons xanthan gum

2 teaspoons GF baking powder

1 teaspoon GF baking soda

½ teaspoon salt

1½ teaspoons ground cinnamon

½ teaspoon ground ginger

½ teaspoon ground nutmeg

Pinch ground cloves (about ⅛ teaspoon)

Cinnamon Whipped Cream (recipe follows)

TO MAKE THE CUPCAKES:

1. Preheat the oven to 350°F. Line standard cupcake tins with paper liners.

2. With an electric mixer, cream together the butter and sugar until fluffy, then add the vanilla.

3. Add the eggs one at a time, mixing to incorporate after each addition.

4. Add the pumpkin and buttermilk, and mix until combined.

5. In a separate bowl, combine the flour, xanthan gum, baking powder, baking soda, salt, cinnamon, ginger, nutmeg, and cloves and mix with a whisk to "sift" the ingredients and break up any lumps.

6. Add the dry ingredients all at once to the sugar mixture and mix for about 10 seconds at medium-low speed to incorporate.

7. Scrape down the sides of the bowl and mix at high speed for about 5 seconds, just until the batter is completely mixed and smooth.

8. Divide the batter evenly among the paper-lined cups. Make the top of the batter as smooth as you can.
9. Bake for 25 minutes.
10. Allow the cupcakes to cool in the tins for 10 minutes, then remove from the tins and let cool completely on a wire rack.
11. While the cupcakes are cooling, make the Cinnamon Whipped Cream.

TO FINISH THE CUPCAKES:
12. Use a large star tip to pipe upward spirals of Cinnamon Whipped Cream onto the cupcakes.

CINNAMON WHIPPED CREAM

2 cups heavy cream
2 tablespoons confectioners' sugar
1 teaspoons GF pure vanilla extract
2 teaspoons ground cinnamon

1. Chill a metal mixing bowl and a whisk or eggbeaters in the freezer for 5 minutes.
2. Pour the cream into the cold bowl and whisk until it starts to thicken.
3. Add the confectioners' sugar, vanilla, and cinnamon, and whisk until soft peaks form. Do not over-mix or the over-whipped cream will take on a curdled appearance. (If this does happen, it's purely a cosmetic issue and won't affect the taste of your whipped cream.)

Hot Fudge Sundae Cupcakes

hot fudge sundae cupcakes

MAKES 24 CUPCAKES

The all-American inspiration for this cupcake was the quintessential hot fudge sundae—a scoop of vanilla ice cream drizzled with hot fudge or chocolate sauce, topped with whipped cream, and finished off with a cherry on top. Here, a vanilla cupcake stands in for the ice cream, but otherwise, we stay true to the spirit of a hot fudge sundae.

¾ cup salted butter (1½ sticks), room temperature

1¾ cups sugar

2 teaspoons GF pure vanilla extract

2 large eggs, room temperature

2 large egg whites, room temperature

1 cup milk

¼ cup sour cream

3 cups Artisan Gluten-Free Flour Blend (page 10)

2 teaspoons xanthan gum

2½ teaspoons GF baking powder

1 teaspoon GF baking soda

½ teaspoon salt

Whipped Cream (recipe follows)

Chocolate Sauce (recipe follows)

24 maraschino cherries

TO MAKE THE CUPCAKES:

1. Preheat the oven to 350°F. Line standard cupcake tins with paper liners.

2. With an electric mixer, cream together the butter and sugar until fluffy, then add the vanilla.

3. Add the eggs and egg whites one at a time, mixing to incorporate after each addition.

4. Add the milk and sour cream and mix until combined.

5. In a separate bowl, combine the flour, xanthan gum, baking powder, baking soda, and salt, and mix with a whisk to "sift" the ingredients and break up any lumps.

6. Add the dry ingredients all at once to the sugar mixture and mix for about 10 seconds at medium-low speed to incorporate.

7. Scrape down the sides of the bowl and mix at high speed for about 5 seconds, just until the batter is completely mixed and smooth.

8. Divide the batter evenly among the paper-lined cups. Make the top of the batter as smooth as you can.

9. Bake for 25 minutes.
10. Allow the cupcakes to cool in the tins for 10 minutes, then remove from the tins and let cool completely on a wire rack.
11. While the cupcakes are cooling, make the Chocolate Sauce and the Whipped Cream.

TO FINISH THE CUPCAKES:

12. Use a large star tip to pipe a spiral of Whipped Cream on the cupcakes.
13. Drizzle the Chocolate Sauce over the Whipped Cream.
14. Garnish each cupcake with a maraschino cherry.

WHIPPED CREAM

2 cups heavy cream
2 tablespoons confectioners' sugar
2 teaspoons GF pure vanilla extract

1. Chill a metal mixing bowl and a whisk or eggbeaters in the freezer for 5 minutes.
2. Pour the cream into the cold bowl and whisk until it starts to thicken.
3. Add the confectioners' sugar and vanilla, and whisk until soft peaks form. Do not over-mix or the over-whipped cream will take on a curdled appearance. (If this does happen, it's purely a cosmetic issue and won't affect the taste of your whipped cream.)

CHOCOLATE SAUCE

⅓ cup sugar
3 tablespoons unsweetened cocoa powder
⅓ cup corn syrup
⅓ cup evaporated milk
2 tablespoons salted butter
¼ teaspoon GF pure vanilla extract
Pinch salt (about ⅛ teaspoon)

1. Whisk together the sugar and cocoa in a medium saucepan.
2. Add the corn syrup, evaporated milk, butter, vanilla, and salt.
3. Cook over medium heat, stirring constantly.
4. Bring the mixture to a full boil and cook, stirring, for 5 minutes or until thick and glossy.
5. Remove the sauce from the heat and let cool to room temperature.

Note: The Chocolate Sauce can be made in advance and stored in the refrigerator in a tightly covered container for up to 1 month. Gently heat the sauce in the microwave or on the stovetop to bring it back to pouring consistency.

Lemon Meringue Cupcake

lemon meringue cupcakes

MAKES 24 CUPCAKES

A cupcake twist on a classic lemon meringue pie, these lemon cupcakes are topped with a basic meringue.

¾ cup salted butter (1½ sticks), room temperature

1¾ cups sugar

1 teaspoon GF pure vanilla extract

2 large eggs, room temperature

2 large egg whites, room temperature

Zest from 1 lemon

¼ cup lemon juice (about 1 lemon, juiced) (see Note, next page)

¼ cup plus 2 tablespoons buttermilk, room temperature

3 cups Artisan Gluten-Free Flour Blend (page 10)

2 teaspoons xanthan gum

2½ teaspoons GF baking powder

1 teaspoon GF baking soda

½ teaspoon salt

Meringue (recipe follows)

TO MAKE THE CUPCAKES:

1. Preheat the oven to 350°F. Line standard cupcake tins with paper liners.

2. With an electric mixer, cream together the butter and sugar until light and fluffy, then add the vanilla.

3. Add the eggs and egg whites one at a time, mixing to incorporate after each addition.

4. Add the zest, lemon juice, and buttermilk, and mix until combined.

5. In a separate bowl, combine the flour, xanthan gum, baking powder, baking soda, and salt, and mix with a whisk to "sift" the ingredients and break up any lumps.

6. Add the dry ingredients all at once to the sugar mixture and mix for about 10 seconds at medium-low speed to incorporate.

7. Scrape down the sides of the bowl and mix at high speed for about 5 seconds, just until the batter is completely mixed and smooth.

8. Divide the batter evenly among the paper-lined cups. Make the top of the batter as smooth as you can.

9. Bake for 25 minutes.

10. Allow the cupcakes to cool in the tins for 10 minutes, then remove from the tins and let cool completely on a wire rack.

TO FINISH THE CUPCAKES:

11. Use a small palette knife to spread the meringue on top of the cupcakes and into sweeping cones.
12. To toast the meringue to a light golden brown, use a kitchen torch and wave the flame back and forth a few inches away from the cupcake. Be careful not to burn the meringue. As you near the lip of the cupcake's paper liner, point the flame upward to avoid burning the paper.

Note: Be sure to zest the lemon first before juicing. Zesting an already-juiced lemon is nearly impossible!

MERINGUE

1⅓ cups plus 1 tablespoon sugar, divided
½ cup water
4 large egg whites
¼ teaspoon salt
2 teaspoons GF pure vanilla extract

1. Mix 1⅓ cups of the sugar and the water in a heavy saucepan. Put a candy thermometer in the sugar mixture and heat to 240°F without stirring.
2. Meanwhile, in a stand mixer using the whisk attachment, whisk the egg whites and salt at medium-high speed until frothy.
3. Add the remaining 1 tablespoon of sugar to the egg whites and whisk until soft peaks form. Turn the mixer off and let the egg whites sit until the sugar comes up to temperature.
4. When sugar mixture reaches 240°F, with the mixer at medium speed, slowly drizzle the hot sugar mixture down the side of the bowl into the beaten egg whites.
5. After all the sugar is added, add the vanilla and continue whisking the mixture about 10 minutes, or until it is cool.

rum raisin cupcakes

MAKES 18 CUPCAKES

A classic pairing—rum and raisin—this cupcake folds rum-soaked raisins into the cake batter, then brushes the cake with a generous amount of Rum Glaze, which really makes the cupcake. The rum flavor is pronounced, but balanced by the sweetness of the raisins.

Melted butter or nonstick cooking
    spray
1 cup raisins
3 tablespoons golden or dark rum
½ cup plus 2 tablespoons salted butter
    (1¼ sticks), room temperature
1¼ cups sugar
1 teaspoon GF pure vanilla extract
3 large eggs, room temperature
½ cup heavy cream
1¾ cups Artisan Gluten-Free Flour
    Blend (page 10)
1 teaspoon xanthan gum
1 teaspoon GF baking powder
½ teaspoon GF baking soda
Pinch salt (about ⅛ teaspoon)

Rum Glaze (recipe follows)

TO MAKE THE CUPCAKES:

1. Preheat the oven to 350°F. Brush standard cupcake tins with the melted butter.

2. Mix the raisins and rum together in a small bowl. Set aside.

3. With an electric mixer, cream together the butter and sugar until light and fluffy, then add the vanilla.

4. Add the eggs one at a time, mixing to incorporate after each addition.

5. Add the cream and rum-raisin mixture, and mix to combine.

6. In a separate bowl, combine the flour, xanthan gum, baking powder, baking soda, and salt, and mix with a whisk to "sift" the ingredients and break up any lumps.

7. Add the dry ingredients all at once to the sugar mixture and mix for about 10 seconds at medium-low speed to incorporate.

8. Scrape down the sides of the bowl and mix at high speed for about 5 seconds, just until the batter is completely mixed and smooth.

9. Line eighteen wells of your cupcake tin with paper liners and divide the

batter evenly among them. Make the top of the batter as smooth as you can. Partially fill any unused wells with water to prevent your cupcake tin from warping in the oven.

10. Bake for 25 minutes.

11. While the cupcakes are baking, make the Rum Glaze.

TO FINISH THE CUPCAKES:

12. Allow the cupcakes to cool in the tins for 2 minutes. Remove from the tins, invert the cupcakes, and put them on a wire rack.

13. Use a pastry brush to brush the Rum Glaze on the tops and sides of the cupcakes (remembering that the bottom of the cupcakes has now become the "top" since they're inverted). Repeat until all the glaze has been absorbed.

14. Serve the cupcakes at room temperature.

RUM GLAZE

½ cup salted butter
1 cup sugar
¼ cup water
½ cup golden or dark rum

1. Mix the butter, sugar, and water in a medium saucepan. Bring the mixture to a boil over high heat, stirring as the butter melts.

2. When the mixture comes to a boil, stop stirring and boil for 5 minutes.

3. Remove from the heat and carefully add the rum all at once. (Some of the rum may flash boil when it hits the pan, spattering for a few seconds.)

4. Stir the mixture until it is smooth.

Rum Raisin Cupcakes

orange dreamsicle cupcakes

MAKES 24 CUPCAKES

Inspired by Popsicle's orange Creamsicles we ate as kids (not to mention the Orange Dream Machine smoothies of Jamba Juice in more recent years), this cupcake blends orange and vanilla flavors to deliver the same flavor profile in the form of an orange cupcake topped with Orange Vanilla Frosting.

¾ cup salted butter (1½ sticks), room temperature

1¾ cups sugar

1 teaspoon GF pure orange extract

2 large eggs, room temperature

2 large egg whites, room temperature

Zest from 2 oranges

½ cup orange juice (about 1 large navel orange, juiced) (see Note, next page)

¼ cup plus 2 tablespoons buttermilk, room temperature

3 cups Artisan Gluten-Free Flour Blend (page 10)

2 teaspoons xanthan gum

2½ teaspoons GF baking powder

1 teaspoon GF baking soda

½ teaspoon salt

Orange Vanilla Frosting (recipe follows)

TO MAKE THE CUPCAKES:

1. Preheat the oven to 350°F. Line standard cupcake tins with paper liners.

2. With an electric mixer, cream together the butter and sugar until light and fluffy, then add the orange extract.

3. Add the eggs and egg whites one at a time, mixing to incorporate after each addition.

4. Add the zest, orange juice, and buttermilk, and mix until combined.

5. In a separate bowl, combine the flour, xanthan gum, baking powder, baking soda, and salt, and mix with a whisk to "sift" the ingredients and break up any lumps.

6. Add the dry ingredients all at once to the sugar mixture and mix for about 10 seconds at medium-low speed to incorporate.

7. Scrape down the sides of the bowl and mix at high speed for about 5 seconds,

just until the batter is completely mixed and smooth.

8. Divide the batter evenly among the paper-lined cups. Make the top of the batter as smooth as you can.

9. Bake for 25 minutes.

10. Allow the cupcakes to cool in the tins for 10 minutes, then remove from the tins and let cool completely on a wire rack.

11. While the cupcakes are cooling, make the Orange Vanilla Frosting.

TO FINISH THE CUPCAKES:

12. Use a large star tip to pipe the Orange Vanilla Frosting in an upward spiral on the cupcakes.

Note: Be sure to zest the orange first before juicing. Zesting an already-juiced orange is nearly impossible!

ORANGE VANILLA FROSTING

1 cup salted butter (2 sticks), room temperature
4 cups confectioners' sugar
¼ cup heavy cream
1 teaspoon GF pure orange extract

Cream together the butter, confectioners' sugar, cream, and orange extract until light and fluffy. (If the frosting is too thick, add more heavy cream, 1 teaspoon at a time, until you have the desired consistency.)

Note: This American buttercream frosting will give these cupcakes the same kind of sweetness we expect from the treats they are based upon, but a lighter, more fresh-tasting frosting option is to use whipped cream flavored with a touch of pure orange extract and garnished with orange zest.

extraordinary

With unexpected twists and extraordinary flavor combinations, these cupcakes go above and beyond the call of cupcake duty. Their added flair, panache, and complexity make them standouts without making them too difficult to execute.

Cookies and Cream Cupcake

cookies and cream cupcakes

This cupcake embodies a chocolate cookie paired with a glass of cold milk. Crumbled Chocolate Cookies in the cupcake—with Vanilla Buttercream topped with more crumbled cookies—really drives home the cookies-and-cream combo. Allow extra time to first bake a batch of Chocolate Cookies (they can be made a day in advance and stored in an airtight container).

¾ cup salted butter (1½ sticks), room temperature

1¾ cups sugar

2 teaspoons GF pure vanilla extract

2 large eggs, room temperature

2 large egg whites, room temperature

1 cup milk

¼ cup sour cream

3 cups Artisan Gluten-Free Flour Blend (page 10)

2 teaspoons xanthan gum

2½ teaspoons GF baking powder

1 teaspoon GF baking soda

½ teaspoon salt

12 Chocolate Cookies (recipe follows)

Vanilla Buttercream (recipe follows)

6 Chocolate Cookies

1. First, make the Chocolate Cookies.

TO MAKE THE CUPCAKES:

2. Preheat the oven to 350°F. Line standard cupcake tins with paper liners.

3. With an electric mixer, cream together the butter and sugar until fluffy, then add the vanilla.

4. Add the eggs and egg whites one at a time, mixing to incorporate after each addition.

5. Add the milk and sour cream and mix until combined.

6. In a separate bowl, combine the flour, xanthan gum, baking powder, baking soda, and salt, and mix with a whisk to "sift" the ingredients and break up any lumps.

7. Add the dry ingredients all at once to the sugar mixture and mix for about

10 seconds at medium-low speed to incorporate.

8. Scrape down the sides of the bowl and mix at high speed for about 5 seconds, just until the batter is completely mixed and smooth.

9. Crumble 12 Chocolate Cookies. Using a rubber spatula, fold into the batter.

10. Divide the batter evenly among the paper-lined cups. Make the top of the batter as smooth as you can.

11. Bake for 25 minutes.

12. Allow the cupcakes to cool in the tins for 10 minutes, then remove from the tins and let cool completely on a wire rack.

13. While the cupcakes are cooling, make the Vanilla Buttercream.

TO FINISH THE CUPCAKES:

14. Use a small palette knife to spread the Vanilla Buttercream on the cupcakes.

15. Crumble the remaining six Chocolate Cookies and sprinkle on top of the buttercream.

CHOCOLATE COOKIES

MAKES 18 COOKIES

8 tablespoons salted butter (1 stick), room temperature

½ cup packed light brown sugar

¼ cup sugar

½ teaspoon GF pure vanilla extract

1 large egg

¾ cup plus 2 tablespoons Artisan Gluten-Free Flour Blend (page 10)

1½ teaspoons xanthan gum

½ teaspoon GF baking soda

½ cup unsweetened cocoa powder

¼ teaspoon salt

1. Preheat the oven to 375°F.
2. Cream together the butter, brown sugar, sugar, and vanilla in a mixer until light and fluffy.
3. Add the egg, mixing until incorporated.
4. Add the flour, xanthan gum, baking soda, cocoa powder, and salt, and mix until well blended.
5. Using a cookie scoop or a teaspoon, drop the dough by rounded teaspoons about 2 inches apart onto an ungreased cookie sheet. You should make 18 cookies.
6. Bake for 10 minutes, or until the edges are set. Let the cookies rest for 5 minutes, then transfer to a wire rack and let cool completely.

VANILLA BUTTERCREAM

1⅓ cups plus 1 tablespoon sugar, divided

½ cup water

4 large egg whites

¼ teaspoon salt

1½ cups salted butter (3 sticks), removed from the refrigerator when you start the buttercream

2 teaspoons GF pure vanilla extract

1. Mix 1⅓ cups of the sugar and the water in a heavy saucepan. Put a candy thermometer in the sugar mixture and heat to 240°F without stirring.
2. Meanwhile, in a stand mixer using a whisk attachment, whisk the egg whites and salt at medium-high speed until frothy.
3. Add the remaining 1 tablespoon of sugar to the egg whites and whisk until soft peaks form. Turn the mixer off and let the egg whites sit until the sugar comes up to temperature.
4. When the sugar mixture reaches 240°F, with the mixer at medium speed, slowly drizzle the hot sugar mixture down the side of the bowl into the beaten egg whites.
5. After all the sugar is added, continue whisking the mixture until it is cool, about 10 minutes.
6. While the egg whites are whisking, cut the butter into tablespoon-size pieces.
7. When the egg whites are cool, leave the mixer running at medium speed and add the butter, 1 tablespoon at a time, allowing enough time for each tablespoon of butter to incorporate after each addition, until all the butter is added.
8. Add the vanilla and mix to combine.
9. Switch to the paddle attachment and mix for an additional 1 or 2 minutes at medium-high speed until the air bubbles are out of the frosting and the frosting is silky smooth.

red, white, and blue cupcakes

MAKES 24 CUPCAKES

This patriotic cupcake is inspired by a red, white, and blue flag cake Kelli's aunt makes every Fourth of July. We incorporate the red, white, and blue theme in two ways—with red, white, and blue layers of cake batter in the cupcake, and with the whipped cream and fresh blueberry and raspberries that top it off. When making this recipe, it is important to have your blueberry and raspberry purees ready to go before making the batter.

1 cup raspberries

1 cup blueberries

¾ cup salted butter (1½ sticks), room
   temperature

1¾ cups sugar

2 teaspoons GF pure vanilla extract

2 large eggs, room temperature

2 large egg whites, room temperature

1 cup milk

¼ cup sour cream

3 cups Artisan Gluten-Free Flour
   Blend (page 10)

2 teaspoons xanthan gum

2½ teaspoons GF baking powder

1 teaspoon GF baking soda

½ teaspoon salt

Whipped Cream (recipe follows)

1 pint fresh raspberries

1 pint fresh blueberries

TO MAKE THE CUPCAKES:

1. Preheat the oven to 350°F. Line standard cupcake tins with paper liners.

2. Puree the 1 cup raspberries and set
   aside.

3. Puree the 1 cup blueberries and set
   aside.

4. With an electric mixer, cream together
   the butter and sugar until fluffy, then
   add the vanilla.

5. Add the eggs and egg whites one at a
   time, mixing to incorporate after each
   addition.

6. Add the milk and sour cream and mix
   until combined.

7. In a separate bowl, combine the flour,
   xanthan gum, baking powder, baking
   soda, and salt, and mix with a whisk
   to "sift" the ingredients and break up
   any lumps.

8. Add the dry ingredients all at once to
   the sugar mixture and mix for about

10 seconds at medium-low speed to incorporate.

9. Scrape down the sides of the bowl and mix at high speed for about 5 seconds, just until the batter is completely mixed and smooth.

10. Divide the batter into thirds and place each third in a separate bowl.

11. Add the pureed raspberries to one bowl of batter and mix to incorporate. Add the pureed blueberries to the second bowl of batter and mix to incorporate. Leave the remaining bowl of batter plain.

12. Place the blueberry batter evenly among the lined cups. Use two fingers moistened with water to smooth the top of the batter.

13. Add a thin layer of the vanilla batter among the cups. Smooth the top of the batter.

14. Finish by spreading the raspberry batter on top of the vanilla layer evenly among the cups. Make the top of the batter as smooth as you can.

15. Bake for 25 minutes.

16. Allow the cupcakes to cool in the tins for 10 minutes, then remove from the tins and let cool completely on a wire rack.

TO FINISH THE CUPCAKES:

17. Spread Whipped Cream on top of the cupcakes and decorate with fresh raspberries and blueberries.

WHIPPED CREAM

2 cups heavy cream
2 tablespoons confectioners' sugar
2 teaspoons GF pure vanilla extract

1. Chill a metal mixing bowl and a whisk or eggbeaters in the freezer for 5 minutes.

2. Pour the cream into the cold bowl and whisk until it starts to thicken.

3. Add the confectioners' sugar and vanilla, and whisk until soft peaks form. Do not over-mix or the over-whipped cream will take on a curdled appearance. (If this does happen, it's purely a cosmetic issue and won't affect the taste of your whipped cream.)

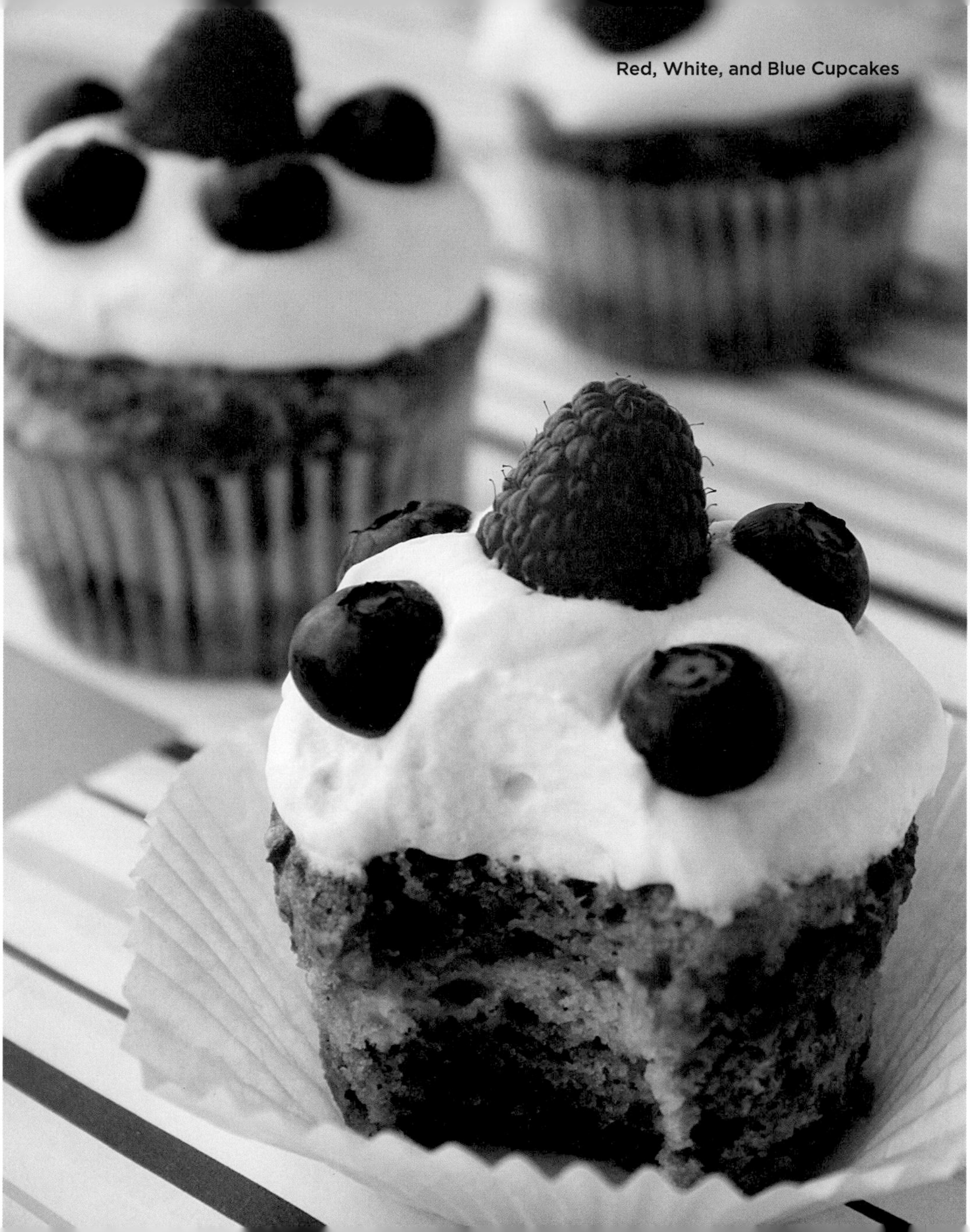
Red, White, and Blue Cupcakes

cannoli cupcakes

A nod to the Sicilian part of Pete's heritage, we base our cupcake on a proper Italian can-nolo, which uses Marsala wine in both a cannolo dough (which is rolled into a tube shape and fried) and in a sweetened ricotta filling. As a cupcake, we begin with a vanilla cake lightly seasoned with cinnamon, and top it with Ricotta Cannoli Filling. Our pièce de résistance, however, is the garnish—a miniature, from-scratch, dyed-in-the-wool gluten-free cannolo. Make the Mini Cannoli Shells fresh immediately before making the cupcakes, and don't fill the cannoli or put them on the cupcakes until you're ready to serve or they will slowly become soggy (as all cannoli—gluten-free and gluten-ous—do). To make the Mini Cannoli Shells, you'll need a handful of either mini metal cannolo tubes or ½-inch diameter, 4-inch long wooden dowels—not necessarily standard kitchen equipment, so plan ahead! Wooden dowels are easily found at home improvement and arts and crafts stores.

¾ cup salted butter (1½ sticks), room temperature

1¾ cups sugar

2 teaspoons GF pure vanilla extract

2 large eggs, room temperature

2 large egg whites, room temperature

1 cup milk

¼ cup sour cream

½ cup Marsala wine

3 cups Artisan Gluten-Free Flour Blend (page 10)

2 teaspoons xanthan gum

2½ teaspoons GF baking powder

1 teaspoon GF baking soda

2 tablespoons cocoa powder

1 teaspoon ground cinnamon

½ teaspoon salt

Mini Cannoli Shells (recipe follows)

Ricotta Cannoli Filling (recipe follows)

½ cup mini chocolate chips, optional

1. First, make the Mini Cannoli Shells.

TO MAKE THE CUPCAKES:

2. Preheat the oven to 350°F. Line standard cupcake tins with paper liners.

3. With an electric mixer, cream together the butter and sugar until light and fluffy, then add the vanilla.

4. Add the eggs and egg whites one at a time, mixing to incorporate after each addition.
5. Add the milk, sour cream, and Marsala, and mix until combined.
6. In a separate bowl, combine the flour, xanthan gum, baking powder, baking soda, cocoa powder, cinnamon, and salt, and mix with a whisk to "sift" the ingredients and break up any lumps.
7. Add the dry ingredients all at once to the sugar mixture and mix for about 10 seconds at medium-low speed to incorporate.
8. Scrape down the sides of the bowl and mix at high speed for about 5 seconds, just until the batter is completely mixed and smooth.
9. Divide the batter evenly among the paper-lined cups. Make the top of the batter as smooth as you can.

10. Bake for 25 minutes.
11. Allow the cupcakes to cool in the tins for 10 minutes, then remove from the tins and let cool completely on a wire rack.
12. While the cupcakes are cooling, make the Ricotta Cannoli Filling.

TO FINISH THE CUPCAKES:

13. Just before you are ready to serve the cupcakes, use a pastry bag with an open tip or a zip-top bag with the bottom corner cut off to fill the prepared Mini Cannoli Shells with Riciotta Cannoli Filling.
14. Use a piping bag with large open tip or a small palette knife to top each cupcake with Ricotta Cannoli Filling.
15. Garnish each cupcake with one mini cannolo.
16. Sprinkle each cupcake with mini chocolate chips, if desired.

MINI CANNOLI SHELLS

MAKES ABOUT 50

1½ cups Artisan Gluten-Free Flour Blend (page 10)

2 tablespoons sugar

Pinch salt (about ⅛ teaspoon)

1 teaspoon xanthan gum

2 tablespoons salted butter, cold

1 large egg

¼ cup Marsala wine

1½ teaspoons white vinegar

1 tablespoon water

1 quart vegetable or canola oil

1 large egg white

Nonstick cooking spray

1. Combine the flour, sugar, salt, and xanthan gum in a bowl.
2. Cut the butter into small pieces and add them to the flour mixture. Work the butter into the flour mixture with your hands until the butter is completely incorporated and the flour resembles small crumbs.
3. In a separate bowl, combine the egg, Marsala, vinegar, and water, whisking with a fork.
4. Add the liquid mixture to the flour mixture, toss it together with the fork, and knead it with your hands until it forms a smooth dough.
5. Divide the dough in half and wrap each half in plastic wrap. Refrigerate for 30 minutes.
6. In a 4-quart saucepan, heat the oil to 365°F.
7. In a small bowl, beat the egg white with a fork.

continued

8. Remove one piece of dough from the refrigerator and roll it out between two pieces of plastic wrap to a thickness of ⅛ inch. Remove the top piece of plastic wrap and use a round cookie cutter or a drinking glass with a 2-inch diameter to cut out circles of dough. (Leftover dough scraps can be combined and re-rolled to make more cannoli shells.)

9. Spray the cannolo tubes or dowels with nonstick cooking spray. (Spraying is necessary only before frying the first batch of cannoli.)

10. Wrap one circle of dough around the prepared tube. Seal the overlapped edge of dough by dipping your finger in the beaten egg white and wiping the egg white on the edge of the dough beneath the overlap, then pressing the upper edge of the overlap onto the bottom edge.

11. Carefully drop one wrapped tube into the oil at a time, being cautious not to put too many in the oil at one time and overcrowd the saucepan.

12. Fry each batch for about 2 minutes, or until golden brown.

13. Remove from the oil and place on paper towels or paper bags to absorb any excess oil. Let the fried cannoli shells cool for about 15 seconds, then use a towel to protect your fingers from the still-hot oil to grasp and slide the shells off the tubes

14. Let the shells cool completely before filling.

RICOTTA CANNOLI FILLING

30 ounces ricotta cheese
1 cup confectioners' sugar
2 teaspoons GF pure vanilla extract

Combine the cheese, confectioners' sugar, and vanilla in a mixing bowl and mix at low speed to combine.

snickerdoodle cupcakes

MAKES 24 CUPCAKES

A snickerdoodle—a sugar cookie rolled in cinnamon sugar before baking—is one of our favorite cookies. Naturally, we just had to turn it into a cupcake, making a vanilla cake lightly seasoned with cinnamon, topping it with cinnamon-sugar-sprinkled Vanilla Buttercream, and, of course, finishing it off with a miniature snickerdoodle cookie topper. If you like snickerdoodle cookies as we do, each bite of this cupcake will bring a smile to your face. When making this recipe, allow extra time to first bake a batch of the gluten-free Mini Snickerdoodle Cookies, or make them ahead of time so you're ready to go.

¾ cup salted butter (1½ sticks), room temperature

1¾ cups sugar

2 teaspoons GF pure vanilla extract

4 large eggs, room temperature

1¼ cups buttermilk, room temperature

3 cups Artisan Gluten-Free Flour Blend (page 10)

2 teaspoons xanthan gum

2½ teaspoons GF baking powder

1 teaspoon GF baking soda

½ teaspoon salt

1 teaspoon ground cinnamon

Vanilla Buttercream (recipe follows)

Mini Snickerdoodle Cookies (recipe follows)

2 teaspoons ground cinnamon

2 tablespoons sugar

1. First, make the Mini Snickerdoodle Cookies.

TO MAKE THE CUPCAKES:

2. Preheat the oven to 350°F. Line standard cupcake tins with paper liners.

3. With an electric mixer, cream together the butter and 1¾ cups of the sugar until light and fluffy, then add the vanilla.

4. Add the eggs one at a time, mixing to incorporate after each addition.

5. Add the buttermilk and mix until combined.

6. In a separate bowl, combine the flour, xanthan gum, baking powder, baking soda, salt, and 1 teaspoon of cinnamon, and mix with a whisk to "sift" the ingredients and break up any lumps.

7. Add the dry ingredients all at once to the sugar mixture, and mix for about 10 seconds at medium-low speed to incorporate.

8. Scrape down the sides of the bowl and mix at high speed for about 5 seconds, just until the batter is completely mixed and smooth.

9. Divide the batter evenly among the paper-lined cups. Make the top of the batter as smooth as you can.

10. Bake for 25 minutes.

11. Allow the cupcakes to cool in the tins for 10 minutes, then remove from the tins and let cool completely on a wire rack.

12. While the cupcakes are cooling, make the Vanilla Buttercream.

TO FINISH THE CUPCAKES:

13. Use a large open tip to pipe a Dairy Queen–type spiral of Vanilla Buttercream on the cupcakes.

14. Place one Mini Snickerdoodle Cookie vertically on top of each buttercream spiral.

15. Combine the 2 tablespoons of sugar and 2 teaspoons of cinnamon and sprinkle over the buttercream.

Snickerdoodle Cupcake

MINI SNICKERDOODLE COOKIES

MAKES ABOUT 50 MINI COOKIES

¾ cup plus 2 tablespoons sugar, divided
½ cup salted butter (1 stick), room temperature
1 large egg
1¼ cups Artisan Gluten-Free Flour Blend (page 10)
1½ teaspoons xanthan gum
1 teaspoon cream of tartar
½ teaspoon GF baking soda
Pinch salt (about ⅛ teaspoon)
2 teaspoons ground cinnamon

1. Preheat the oven to 400°F.
2. With an electric mixer, cream together ¾ cup of the sugar and the butter until light and fluffy.
3. Stir in the egg, mixing to incorporate.
4. Stir in the flour, xanthan gum, cream of tartar, baking soda, and salt.
5. In a small bowl, mix the remaining 2 tablespoons of sugar and the cinnamon.
6. Using a spoon, scoop the dough into ½-teaspoon-size scoops. Roll the dough between the palms of your hands to make a ball, and roll the balls in the cinnamon sugar.
7. Place the balls on an ungreased cookie sheet 1 inch apart. Gently press on each ball to flatten slightly.
8. Bake for 5 to 6 minutes, until slightly brown at the edges. Let rest on the cookie sheet for 2 minutes, then transfer to a wire rack to cool completely.

VANILLA BUTTERCREAM

1⅓ cups plus 1 tablespoon sugar, divided

½ cup water

4 large egg whites

¼ teaspoon salt

1½ cups salted butter (3 sticks), removed from the refrigerator when you start the buttercream

2 teaspoons GF pure vanilla extract

1. Mix 1⅓ cups of the sugar and the water in a heavy saucepan. Put a candy thermometer in the mixture and heat to 240°F without stirring.
2. Meanwhile, in a stand mixer using the whisk attachment, whisk the egg whites and salt at medium-high speed until frothy.
3. Add the remaining 1 tablespoon of sugar to the egg whites and whisk until soft peaks form. Turn the mixer off and let the egg whites sit until the sugar mixture comes up to temperature.
4. When the sugar mixture reaches 240°F, with the mixer at medium speed, slowly drizzle the hot sugar mixture down the side of the bowl into the beaten egg whites.
5. After all the sugar is added, continue whisking the mixture until it is cool, about 10 minutes.
6. While the egg whites are whisking, cut the butter into tablespoon-size pieces.
7. When the egg whites are cool, leave the mixer running at medium speed and add the butter, 1 tablespoon at a time, allowing enough time for each tablespoon of butter to incorporate after each addition, until all the butter is added.
8. Add the vanilla and mix to combine.
9. Switch to the paddle attachment and mix for an additional 1 to 2 minutes at medium-high speed until the air bubbles are out of the frosting and the frosting is silky smooth.

Dulce de Leche Cupcake

dulce de leche cupcakes

MAKES 24 CUPCAKES

Popular throughout Latin America—and with similar relatives in other countries, such as France—dulce de leche is a milk caramel made by slowly heating milk sweetened with sugar. Over the centuries its origin has been the subject of many stories, some based perhaps on a kernel of truth, but otherwise shrouded in legend and the sands of time. These days everyone seems to agree on one thing, though: it's delicious. For our cupcake, we start with a brown sugar cupcake, drizzle a generous portion of from-scratch dulce over the top, and finish it off with a dollop of Dulce de Leche Whipped Cream. If making dulce from scratch, plan ahead and allow several hours for the process before starting the cupcakes, or make the Dulce de Leche in advance.

¾ cup salted butter (1½ sticks), room temperature

1¾ cups packed brown sugar

2 teaspoons GF pure vanilla extract

4 large eggs, room temperature

1¼ cups buttermilk, room temperature

3 cups Artisan Gluten-Free Flour Blend (page 10)

2 teaspoons xanthan gum

2½ teaspoons GF baking powder

1 teaspoon GF baking soda

½ teaspoon salt

Dulce de Leche (recipe follows) (see Note, next page)

Dulce de Leche Whipped Cream (recipe follows)

1. First, make the Dulce de Leche.

TO MAKE THE CUPCAKES:

2. Preheat the oven to 350°F. Line standard cupcake tins with paper liners.

3. With an electric mixer, cream together the butter and brown sugar until light and fluffy, then add the vanilla.

4. Add the eggs one at a time, mixing to incorporate after each addition.

5. Add the buttermilk and mix until combined.

6. In a separate bowl, combine the flour, xanthan gum, baking powder, baking soda, and salt, and mix with a whisk to "sift" the ingredients and break up any lumps.

7. Add the dry ingredients all at once to the sugar mixture and mix for about 10 seconds at medium-low speed to incorporate.

8. Scrape down the sides of the bowl and mix at high speed for about 5 seconds, just until the batter is completely mixed and smooth.

9. Divide the batter evenly among the paper-lined cups. Make the top of the batter as smooth as you can.

10. Bake for 25 minutes.

11. Allow the cupcakes to cool in the tins for 10 minutes, then remove from the tins and let cool completely on a wire rack.

12. While the cupcakes are cooling, make the Dulce de Leche Whipped Cream.

TO FINISH THE CUPCAKES:

13. Drizzle the top of each cupcake with a generous portion of Dulce de Leche, enough so the top of the cupcake is covered and the dulce just begins to run down the sides of the cake.

14. Top each cupcake with a dollop of Dulce de Leche Whipped Cream.

Note: For a quick and easy alternative, you can also use store-bought dulce de leche (one 14 to 16-ounce can will do it).

DULCE DE LECHE WHIPPED CREAM

1 cup heavy cream
¼ cup Dulce de Leche

1. Chill a metal mixing bowl and a whisk or eggbeaters in the freezer for 5 minutes.

2. Pour the cream into the cold bowl and whisk until it starts to thicken.

3. Add the Dulce de Leche and whisk until soft peaks form. Do not over-mix or the over-whipped cream will take on a curdled appearance. (If this does happen, it's purely a cosmetic issue and won't affect the taste of your whipped cream.)

DULCE DE LECHE

3 cups 2-percent milk
1 cup half-and-half
1½ cups sugar
½ teaspoon GF baking soda
1 teaspoon GF pure vanilla extract

1. Combine the milk, half-and-half, and sugar in a 4- to 5-quart saucepan. Bring to a simmer over medium-high heat.
2. Stir in the baking soda and turn the heat down to medium-low.
3. Continue to cook the mixture uncovered until it is a deep brown color, about 3 hours, stirring once or twice an hour until reduced to about 1½ cups of liquid. About once per hour, remove the foam from the top of the dulce and discard it.
4. After about 3 hours, remove from the heat and stir in the vanilla.
5. Strain the mixture through a fine metal mesh strainer.
6. Let it cool to room temperature. If you find that your room temperature dulce de leche is too runny, return it to the heat to reduce and thicken further. If you are not using it immediately, cover and store in the refrigerator.

French Toast Cupcake

french toast cupcakes

French toast casserole is a favorite breakfast in our family. It typically combines leftover bread with eggs, milk, cinnamon, sugar, and vanilla to make a kind of bread pudding that bakes in the oven. It then gets drizzled with a bit of pure maple syrup. Despite its name, however, we seldom use toast—or bread in general—to make it. Instead, we opt for pancakes, which yield a great, light texture. As a cupcake we add a Maple Cream Cheese Frosting, but otherwise, these mini casseroles stay true to their big brother.

½ cup salted butter (1 stick), melted plus additional for the cupcake tins (or use nonstick cooking spray)

8 cups GF pancakes, cut or torn into 1-inch pieces (recipe follows) (see Note, next page)

4 large eggs

3 cups milk

2 tablespoons sugar

4 teaspoons ground cinnamon

2 teaspoons GF pure vanilla extract

Maple Cream Cheese Frosting (recipe follows)

1 teaspoon ground cinnamon

1. First, make the pancakes.

TO MAKE THE CUPCAKES:

2. Preheat the oven to 350°F. Brush the cupcake tins with the melted butter.

3. Place the pancakes in a large bowl. Drizzle ½ cup of the melted butter over the pancakes and toss to coat.

4. In a separate bowl, whisk together the eggs, milk, sugar, 4 teaspoons of cinnamon, and vanilla.

5. Pour the egg mixture over the pancakes.

6. Divide the batter evenly among the prepared cups. Each cup should be filled almost to the top.

7. Bake for 30 minutes.

8. Allow the cupcakes to cool in the tins for 10 minutes.

9. Carefully run the tip of a thin knife around each cupcake to separate the cake from the edges of the tin. Turn

the tins over onto wire racks so the cupcakes drop out. Allow them to cool completely.

10. While the cupcakes are cooling, make the Maple Cream Cheese Frosting.

TO FINISH THE CUPCAKES:

11. Use a small palette knife to spread the Maple Cream Cheese Frosting on top of the cupcakes.

12. Using a fine mesh metal sieve, dust the frosting with the 1 teaspoon of cinnamon.

Note: If you have gluten-free bread on hand and don't want to make the pancakes, you can substitute the bread into the recipe, though we prefer the taste and texture of these pancakes.

MAPLE CREAM CHEESE FROSTING

12 ounces cream cheese, room temperature
³/₄ cup plus 2 tablespoons salted butter (1³/₄ sticks), room temperature
½ cup pure maple syrup
2½ cups confectioners' sugar
1 teaspoon GF pure maple extract

1. With an electric mixer, cream together the cream cheese and butter until completely incorporated.

2. Add the maple syrup, confectioners' sugar, and maple extract, and mix until smooth and of spreading consistency. (Additional confectioners' sugar can be added, if needed, to make a thicker frosting.)

PANCAKES

2 cups Artisan Gluten-Free Flour Blend (page 10)
2 tablespoons sugar
4 teaspoons GF baking powder
½ teaspoon salt
2 large eggs
2 cups milk
2 teaspoons GF pure vanilla extract
**¼ cup salted butter (½ stick), melted, plus additional for the griddle or skillet
(or use nonstick cooking spray)**

1. Mix the flour, sugar, baking powder, and salt in a large bowl.
2. Add the eggs, milk, and vanilla, and mix.
3. Add ¼ cup of the melted butter and mix, just until the ingredients are combined.
4. Heat a griddle to medium-high. Grease with the melted butter.
5. Using a 2-ounce ladle, pour the batter into rounds on the hot griddle. Cook until bubbles have formed on the surface of each pancake and the underside is golden brown.
6. Flip and cook until the other side is also golden brown.
7. Repeat steps 5 and 6 until you've used up all the batter.

Mojito Cupcake

mojito cupcakes

MAKES 24 CUPCAKES

We've always enjoyed this Cuban highball drink made with lime, mint, rum, sugar, and sparkling water (at least since we've been of legal drinking age . . .). Though some were skeptical at first, we've since earned many converts to this cupcake, with its balance of mint and lime. Its flavor comes from freshly squeezed lime juice and chopped mint leaves, giving it a clean, fresh taste.

¾ cup salted butter (1½ sticks), room temperature

1¾ cups sugar

2 teaspoons GF pure vanilla extract

4 large eggs, room temperature

1 cup buttermilk, room temperature

½ cup light rum

Zest of 1 lime

¼ cup lime juice (about 1 lime, juiced) (see Note, next page)

2 tablespoons minced mint

3 cups Artisan Gluten-Free Flour Blend (page 10)

2 teaspoons xanthan gum

2½ teaspoons GF baking powder

1 teaspoon GF baking soda

½ teaspoon salt

Lime Mint Buttercream (recipe follows)

2 to 3 limes, sliced thin

24 mint sprigs

TO MAKE THE CUPCAKES:

1. Preheat the oven to 350°F. Line standard cupcake tins with paper liners.

2. With an electric mixer, cream together the butter and sugar until light and fluffy, then add the vanilla.

3. Add the eggs one at a time, mixing to incorporate after each addition.

4. Add the buttermilk, rum, zest, and lime juice, and mix until combined.

5. In a separate bowl, combine the flour, xanthan gum, baking powder, baking soda, and salt, and mix with a whisk to "sift" the ingredients and break up any lumps.

6. Add the dry ingredients all at once to the sugar mixture, and mix for about

10 seconds at medium-low speed to incorporate.

7. Scrape down the sides of the bowl and mix at high speed for about 5 seconds, just until the batter is completely mixed and smooth.

8. Divide the batter evenly among the paper-lined cups. Make the top of the batter as smooth as you can.

9. Bake for 25 minutes.

10. Allow the cupcakes to cool in the tins for 10 minutes, then remove from the tins and let cool completely on a wire rack.

11. While the cupcakes are cooling, make the Lime Mint Buttercream.

TO FINISH THE CUPCAKES:

12. Use a large star tip to pipe the Lime Mint Buttercream in an upward spiral on the cupcakes.

13. Garnish with 1 lime slice and 1 fresh mint sprig.

Note: Be sure to zest the lime first before juicing. Zesting an already-juiced lime is nearly impossible!

LIME MINT BUTTERCREAM

1⅓ cups plus 1 tablespoon sugar, divided

½ cup water

15 mint sprigs (about 30 leaves)

4 large egg whites

¼ teaspoon salt

1½ cups salted butter (3 sticks), removed from the refrigerator when you start the buttercream

¼ cup lime juice (about 1 lime, juiced)

Zest of 1 lime

¼ cup mint, finely chopped

1. Mix 1⅓ cups of the sugar and the water in a heavy saucepan. Add the mint sprigs. Put a candy thermometer in the sugar mixture and heat to 240°F without stirring.
2. Meanwhile, in a stand mixer using the whisk attachment, whisk the egg whites and salt at medium-high speed until frothy.
3. Add the remaining 1 tablespoon of sugar to the egg whites and whisk until soft peaks form. Turn the mixer off and let the egg whites sit until the sugar comes up to temperature.
4. When the sugar mixture reaches 240°F, carefully remove the mint sprigs and any loose leaves, and with the mixer at medium speed, slowly drizzle the hot sugar mixture down the side of the bowl into the beaten egg whites.
5. After all the sugar is added, continue whisking the mixture until it is cool, about 10 minutes.
6. While the egg whites are whisking, cut the butter into tablespoon-size pieces.
7. When the egg whites are cool, leave the mixer running at medium speed and add the butter, 1 tablespoon at a time, allowing enough time for each tablespoon of butter to incorporate after each addition, until all the butter is added.
8. Switch to the paddle attachment, add the lime juice, zest, and chopped mint, and mix at medium speed for an additional 1 to 2 minutes until the air bubbles are out of the frosting and the frosting is silky smooth.

Poached Pearfection Cupcake

poached pearfection cupcakes

Unabashedly inspired by our wedding cake, our cupcake features a poached pear and vanilla bean cake topped with a Salted Caramel Buttercream. The flavor of the pear in the cake is subtle, but the white wine–poached pear lends a sweetness as well as a tender, moist crumb. The Salted Caramel Buttercream is surprising—it starts sweet, but finishes slightly salty.

¾ cup salted butter (1½ sticks), room temperature

1½ cups sugar

2 teaspoons GF pure vanilla extract

4 large eggs, room temperature

2 Poached Pears, pureed (recipe follows)

½ cup poaching liquid (see Poached Pears recipe)

¾ cup buttermilk, room temperature

3¼ cups Artisan Gluten-Free Flour Blend (page 10)

2 teaspoons xanthan gum

2½ teaspoons GF baking powder

1 teaspoon GF baking soda

½ teaspoon salt

Salted Caramel Buttercream (recipe follows)

1. First, make the Poached Pears.

TO MAKE THE CUPCAKES:

2. Preheat the oven to 350°F. Line standard cupcake tins with paper liners.

3. With an electric mixer, cream together the butter and sugar until light and fluffy, then add the vanilla.

4. Add the eggs one at a time, mixing to incorporate after each addition.

5. Add the poached pear puree and poaching liquid, and mix to combine.

6. Add the buttermilk and mix.

7. In a separate bowl, combine the flour, xanthan gum, baking powder, baking soda, and salt, and mix with a whisk to "sift" the ingredients and break up any lumps.

8. Add the dry ingredients all at once to the sugar mixture and mix for about 10 seconds at medium-low speed to incorporate.

9. Scrape down the sides of the bowl and mix at high speed for about 5 seconds,

just until the batter is completely mixed and smooth.

10. Divide the batter evenly among the paper-lined cups. Make the top of the batter as smooth as you can.

11. Bake for 25 minutes.

12. Allow the cupcakes to cool in the tins for 10 minutes, then remove from the tins and let cool completely on a wire rack.

13. While the cupcakes are cooling, make the Salted Caramel Buttercream.

TO FINISH THE CUPCAKES:

14. Use a small palette knife to spread the Salted Caramel Buttercream on the cupcakes.

POACHED PEARS

2 cups white wine (light in flavor, such as a pinot grigio . . . no oaked chardonnay, please!)

½ cup sugar

1 vanilla bean

2 pears, peeled, cored, and quartered (Bosc or Anjou pears are best)

1. Combine the wine and sugar in a medium saucepan.

2. Split the vanilla bean in half and scrape out all the pulp and seeds. Add the split bean, pulp, and seeds to the wine.

3. Heat the mixture over medium-high heat and bring to a boil.

4. Add the pears and turn the heat down to medium-low. Cover and cook for 40 minutes, or until the pears are very soft.

5. Remove the pears and the split vanilla bean from the wine mixture, and simmer for an additional 20 minutes, uncovered, to reduce the liquid to approximately ½ cup.

6. Reserve both the pears and the liquid for the cupcakes.

SALTED CARAMEL BUTTERCREAM

¾ cup plus ½ cup sugar, divided

3 tablespoons water

¾ cup heavy cream

½ teaspoon GF pure vanilla extract

4 large egg whites

1½ cups salted butter (3 sticks), removed from the refrigerator when you start the buttercream

1. In a medium saucepan, stir together ¾ cup of the sugar and the water. Cook the mixture over high heat, without stirring, until it is a golden brown. (If the sugar starts to brown in just one area, gently swirl the pan; it will agitate the mixture just enough to distribute the heat. Do not stir.) If the sugar is pale yellow, it needs to cook a little longer; if it is dark brown, it has cooked too long.

2. As soon as the mixture is golden brown, carefully add the cream all at once and pull your hand back. (The heat of the sugar will instantly boil some of the cream, which might spatter for a few seconds.) Stir vigorously and cook for about 2 minutes, or until the sugar and cream melt together and create a beautiful, smooth texture.

3. Remove from the heat, add the vanilla, stir, and set the caramel aside to cool.

4. In the metal bowl of a stand mixer, combine the egg whites, salt, and remaining ½ cup of sugar. Place the bowl over a saucepan of simmering water and put a candy thermometer in the mixture.

5. Heat the mixture while whisking by hand to 140°F.

6. When the mixture reaches 140°F, put the bowl on the stand mixer and, using the whisk attachment, whisk at medium speed for about 10 minutes, or until the egg whites are cool.

7. While the egg whites are cooling, cut the butter into tablespoon-size pieces.

8. When the egg whites are cool, add the butter, 1 tablespoon at a time, mixing to incorporate after each addition until all the butter is added.

9. Switch to the paddle attachment, add the reserved caramel, and mix at medium speed for an additional 1 to 2 minutes until the air bubbles are out of the frosting and the frosting is silky smooth.

Tiramisu Cupcake

tiramisu cupcakes

MAKES 24 CUPCAKES

Tiramisu is a popular Italian dessert built upon ladyfingers (light finger-size sponge cakes) soaked in coffee and paired with a sweetened mascarpone-coffee filling. The dessert is usually finished off with a liberal dusting of cocoa powder, whose natural bitterness balances the sweetness of the mascarpone. Our cupcake is essentially an homage to a true tiramisu, yet takes on its own character.

⅓ cup sugar

3 large eggs

4 large egg yolks

Pinch salt (about ⅛ teaspoon)

¼ cup salted butter (½ stick)

½ cup milk

2 teaspoons GF pure vanilla extract

1¾ cups plus 2 tablespoons Artisan Gluten-Free Flour Blend (page 10)

2 teaspoons GF baking powder

Espresso Syrup (recipe follows)

Mascarpone Topping (recipe follows)

1 ounce semi-sweet chocolate, bar form

TO MAKE THE CUPCAKES:

1. Preheat the oven to 350°F. Line standard cupcake tins with paper liners.

2. In a stand mixer metal bowl (or a heat-proof metal bowl if using a handheld electric mixer), whisk together the sugar, eggs, egg yolks, and salt. Place the mixture over a saucepan of simmering water. Make sure the water does not touch the bottom of the bowl.

3. Place a thermometer in the egg mixture and whisk over the heat until the mixture reaches 110°F.

4. Use the whisk attachment of a stand mixer (or the beaters of a handheld mixer) and whisk at high speed until the eggs are very light and thick, about 5 minutes.

5. While the eggs are whisking, in a small saucepan heat the butter and milk over medium heat, just until the butter melts. Remove from the heat and add the vanilla. Set aside.

6. In a small bowl, whisk the flour and baking powder together.

7. With a rubber spatula, fold the flour mixture into the eggs.

8. Fold the butter mixture in, just until incorporated. Do not over-mix.
9. Divide the batter evenly among the paper-lined cups. Bake for 20 minutes.
10. Meanwhile, prepare the Espresso Syrup.
11. While the cupcakes are still hot and in the tins, use a pastry brush to brush the Espresso Syrup on the cupcakes. Let the syrup soak into the cakes; repeat until you've used up the syrup. Let the cupcakes cool in the tins.
12. While the cupcakes are cooling, make the Mascarpone Frosting.

TO FINISH THE CUPCAKES:
13. When the cupcakes are cool, remove from the tins.
14. Use a small palette knife to spread the Mascarpone Frosting on the cupcakes.
15. With a cheese grater, shave the chocolate bar.
16. Garnish with the shaved chocolate.

ESPRESSO SYRUP

3 tablespoons coffee liqueur
3 tablespoons hot water
3 teaspoons espresso powder

In a small bowl, mix together the coffee liqueur, hot water, and espresso powder until the espresso powder is dissolved.

MASCARPONE FROSTING

1 cup heavy cream
16 ounces mascarpone cheese
½ teaspoon salt
½ cup confectioners' sugar
¼ cup coffee liqueur
2 teaspoons GF pure vanilla extract
2 ounces semi-sweet chocolate, finely shaved (via Microplane grater)

1. In a small bowl, whisk the cream until it stands in stiff peaks. Set aside.
2. In a separate bowl, whisk together the mascarpone, salt, confectioners' sugar, coffee liqueur, vanilla, and chocolate until the mixture is smooth.
3. Use a rubber spatula to fold the whisked cream into the mascarpone mixture.
4. Cover and refrigerate.

Maple Madness Cupcake

maple madness cupcakes

MAKES 24 CUPCAKES

This cupcake is maple, maple, and more maple. It's a maple-infused cupcake topped with Maple Cream Cheese Frosting and finished with a tiny maple sugar candy, if desired. Despite using a full cup of pure maple syrup in the batter, the moist cake has a surprisingly subtle maple flavor (which we boost a bit with some pure maple extract), but that's more than made up for with the intensely maple-flavored frosting.

¾ cup salted butter (1½ sticks), room temperature

½ cup packed brown sugar

1 teaspoon GF pure vanilla extract

1 teaspoon GF pure maple extract

2 large eggs, room temperature

2 large egg whites, room temperature

1 cup pure maple syrup (ideally, Grade B)

¾ cup milk

¼ cup sour cream

3 cups Artisan Gluten-Free Flour Blend (page 10)

2 teaspoons xanthan gum

2½ teaspoons GF baking powder

1 teaspoon GF baking soda

½ teaspoon salt

Maple Cream Cheese Frosting (recipe follows)

Ground cinnamon or small maple sugar candies (optional)

TO MAKE THE CUPCAKES:

1. Preheat the oven to 350°F. Line standard cupcake tins with paper liners.

2. With an electric mixer, cream together the butter and sugar until light and fluffy, then add the vanilla and maple extract.

3. Add the eggs and egg whites one at a time, mixing to incorporate after each addition.

4. Add the syrup, milk, and sour cream, and mix until combined.

5. In a separate bowl, combine the flour, xanthan gum, baking powder, baking soda, and salt, and mix with a whisk to "sift" the ingredients and break up any lumps.

6. Add the dry ingredients all at once to the sugar mixture and mix for about 10 seconds at medium-low speed to incorporate.

7. Scrape down the sides of the bowl and mix at high speed for about 5 seconds, just until the batter is completely mixed and smooth.

8. Divide the batter evenly among the paper-lined cups. Make the top of the batter as smooth as you can.

9. Bake for 25 minutes.

10. Allow the cupcakes to cool in the tins for 10 minutes, then remove from the tins and let cool completely on a wire rack.

11. While the cupcakes are cooling, make the Maple Cream Cheese Frosting.

TO FINISH THE CUPCAKES:

12. Use a small palette knife to spread the Maple Cream Cheese Frosting on top of each cupcake, leaving the top of the frosting flat and smooth.

13. Choose a maple leaf–shaped cookie cutter that's smaller than the diameter of the cupcakes and trace its shape onto a piece of heavyweight paper or card stock. Use scissors to carefully cut out the leaf. Retain the leaf-shaped cutout and recycle the surrounding excess paper.

14. Gently center the leaf on the top of each cupcake and, using a small fine mesh strainer, dust each cupcake with the cinnamon. (If using maple candies, omit the cinnamon and center a small maple candy on each cupcake.)

Note: You could also do the photographic negative of the maple cutout. Trace a maple leaf-shaped cookie cutter onto heavyweight paper or card stock. Instead of scissors, use a sharp hobby knife to cut out the maple leaf shape without requiring an in-cut from the edge of the paper. Then recycle the leaf-shaped paper and retain the surrounding paper with the leaf-shaped hole in the center. Use this as your pattern for dusting the cinnamon. Or, retain both the leaf-shaped paper *and* the surrounding paper with leaf-shaped hole, which gives you two options for finishing your cupcakes.

MAPLE CREAM CHEESE FROSTING

12 ounces cream cheese, room temperature

¾ cup plus 2 tablespoons salted butter, (1½ sticks plus 2 tablespoons) room temperature

½ cup pure maple syrup (ideally, Grade B)

2½ cups confectioners' sugar

1 teaspoon GF pure maple extract

1. With an electric mixer, cream together the cream cheese and butter until completely incorporated.
2. Add the maple syrup, confectioners' sugar, and maple extract, and mix until smooth and of spreading consistency. (Additional confectioners' sugar can be added, as needed, to make a thicker frosting.)

a guide to refined-sugar-free, dairy-free, egg-free, and vegan baking

*E*very recipe in this book is gluten-free. But if you have additional dietary restrictions—such as avoiding refined sugar, dairy, or eggs—this section will become your best friend for making the recipes. We've developed alternative versions of the fundamental recipes of vanilla and chocolate cake bases and vanilla and chocolate frostings to suit many diets. More than 80 percent of the book's recipes, are built upon these fundamental recipes, but with modifications such as supplemental fruit, puree, or other flavorings. **If you make the following base cake and frosting recipes, and add any supplemental flavors called for in the recipe of the specific cupcake you want, you'll enjoy delicious cupcakes that also match your dietary needs!**

Here's what you'll find in the guidelines that follow:

IF YOU ARE REFINED-SUGAR-FREE

- A vanilla and chocolate Italian buttercream

- A chocolate ganache
- Two versions of our standard high-ratio vanilla cake
- Two versions of our buttermilk vanilla cake
- Two versions of our chocolate cake

IF YOU ARE DAIRY-FREE

- An American buttercream
- An Italian meringue
- A chocolate ganache
- A standard high-ratio vanilla cake
- A buttermilk vanilla cake
- A chocolate cake

IF YOU ARE EGG-FREE

- An American buttercream (naturally egg-free)
- A chocolate ganache (also naturally egg-free)
- A standard high-ratio vanilla cake
- A buttermilk vanilla cake
- A chocolate cake

IF YOU ARE VEGAN

- An American buttercream
- A chocolate ganache
- A standard high-ratio vanilla cake
- A buttermilk vanilla cake
- A chocolate cake

Note: For the recipes that follow, we've listed all the "standard" ingredients in the left-hand column for easy reference. Then, in the columns to the right (which may include refined-sugar-free, dairy-free, egg-free, and vegan), we've listed only ingredients requiring substitution. If an ingredient remains unchanged between the original version and the alternative version, we've left that space blank.

frostings

AMERICAN BUTTERCREAM (POWDERED SUGAR FROSTING)

ORIGINAL RECIPE (NATURALLY EGG-FREE)	DAIRY-FREE AND VEGAN
1 cup salted butter	1½ cups non-hydrogenated vegan shortening (e.g., Earth Balance Vegan Buttery Sticks)
4 cups confectioners' sugar	3¾ cups confectioners' sugar
¼ cup heavy cream	For vanilla: 3 tablespoons soy milk For chocolate: ¼ cup + 2 tablespoons soy milk
	For vanilla and chocolate: 3 teaspoons GF vanilla
	For chocolate: ¾ cup unsweetened cocoa

ITALIAN BUTTERCREAM

ORIGINAL RECIPE	REFINED-SUGAR-FREE	DAIRY-FREE (ITALIAN MERINGUE)
1 ⅓ cups + 1 tablespoon sugar, divided	1 ⅓ cups light agave nectar	
½ cup water	Omit the water.	
4 egg whites		
¼ teaspoon salt		
1½ cups salted butter		Omit the butter and stop the recipe when you've made the meringue.
For vanilla and chocolate: 2 teaspoons GF vanilla		
For chocolate: 8 ounces semi-sweet chocolate	For chocolate: ¼ cup unsweetened cocoa	

CHOCOLATE GANACHE

ORIGINAL RECIPE (NATURALLY EGG-FREE)	REFINED-SUGAR-FREE, DAIRY-FREE, AND VEGAN
8 ounces bittersweet chocolate	5 ounces unsweetened chocolate
¾ cup heavy cream	¾ cup + 3 tablespoons light agave nectar
	¼ cup + 1 tablespoon soy milk

cupcakes

STANDARD HIGH-RATIO VANILLA CAKE

Use either this recipe or the Buttermilk Vanilla Cake recipe that follows to make alternate versions of the vanilla cupcakes in the Classics chapter, all the cupcakes in the Fruity chapter, the Pistachio Cupcakes, and all the cupcakes in the Sweet Surprises chapter, the Old Faithful chapter (except Gingerbread, Pumpkin Spice, and Rum Raisin), and the Extraordinary chapter (except French Toast and Tiramisu).

ORIGINAL RECIPE	REFINED-SUGAR-FREE VERSION 1: AGAVE NECTAR	REFINED-SUGAR-FREE VERSION 2: BROWN RICE SYRUP	DAIRY-FREE	EGG-FREE	VEGAN
¾ cup salted butter			¾ cup non-hydrogenated vegan shortening (e.g., Earth Balance Vegan Buttery Sticks)		¾ cup non-hydrogenated vegan shortening (e.g., Earth Balance Vegan Buttery Sticks)
1 ¾ cups sugar	1 cup + 3 tablespoons light agave nectar	2 cups + 3 tablespoons brown rice syrup			
2 teaspoons GF vanilla					
2 eggs				4 tablespoons ground flax meal whisked in 1 cup water; let sit for 2 minutes before using	4 tablespoons ground flax meal whisked in 1 cup water; let sit for 2 minutes before using
2 egg whites					
1 cup milk	¾ cup milk	½ cup + 1 tablespoon milk	1 ¼ cups soy milk		1 ¼ cups soy milk
¼ cup sour cream			¼ cup dairy-free sour cream (e.g., Tofutti non-hydrogenated soy sour cream)		¼ cup dairy-free sour cream (e.g., Tofutti non-hydrogenated soy sour cream)
3 cups GF flour					
2 teaspoons xanthan gum					
2 ½ teaspoons GF baking powder					
1 teaspoon GF baking soda					
½ teaspoon salt					

BUTTERMILK VANILLA CAKE

ORIGINAL RECIPE	REFINED-SUGAR-FREE VERSION 1: AGAVE NECTAR	REFINED-SUGAR-FREE VERSION 2: BROWN RICE SYRUP	DAIRY-FREE	EGG-FREE	VEGAN
¾ cup salted butter			¾ cup non-hydrogenated vegan shortening (e.g., Earth Balance Vegan Buttery Sticks)		¾ cup non-hydrogenated vegan shortening (e.g., Earth Balance Vegan Buttery Sticks)
1¾ cups sugar	1 cup + 3 tablespoons light agave nectar	2 cups + 3 tablespoons brown rice syrup			
2 teaspoons GF vanilla					
4 eggs				4 tablespoons ground flax meal whisked in 1 cup water; let sit for 2 minutes before using	4 tablespoons ground flax meal whisked in 1 cup water; let sit for 2 minutes before using
1¼ cups buttermilk	1 cup buttermilk	¾ cup + 1 tablespoon buttermilk	1½ cups acidified almond or soy milk (add 1½ tablespoons white distilled vinegar to 1½ cups dairy-free milk)		1½ cups acidified almond or soy milk (add 1½ tablespoons white distilled vinegar to 1½ cups dairy-free milk)
3 cups GF flour					
2 teaspoons xanthan gum					
2½ teaspoons GF baking powder					
1 teaspoon GF baking soda					
½ teaspoon salt					

CHOCOLATE CAKE

Use this recipe to make alternate versions of Chocolate Cupcakes with Vanilla Frosting and all of the cupcakes in the Chocoholic chapter (except Flourless Chocolate Cupcakes).

ORIGINAL RECIPE	REFINED-SUGAR-FREE VERSION 1: AGAVE NECTAR	REFINED-SUGAR-FREE VERSION 2: BROWN RICE SYRUP	DAIRY-FREE	EGG-FREE	VEGAN
1 cup salted butter			1 cup non-hydrogenated vegan shortening (e.g., Earth Balance Vegan Buttery Sticks)		1 cup non-hydrogenated vegan shortening (e.g., Earth Balance Vegan Buttery Sticks)
1 cup water	¾ cup water	¼ cup water			
½ cup unsweetened cocoa					
2 cups sugar	1⅓ cups light agave nectar	2½ cups brown rice syrup			
1 teaspoon GF vanilla					
2 eggs				2 tablespoons ground flax meal whisked in ½ cup water; let sit for 2 minutes before using	2 tablespoons ground flax meal whisked in ½ cup water; let sit for 2 minutes before using
1 cup sour cream			1 cup dairy-free sour cream (e.g., Tofutti non-hydrogenated soy sour cream)		1 cup dairy-free sour cream (e.g., Tofutti non-hydrogenated soy sour cream)
2½ cups GF flour					
2 teaspoons xanthan gum					
1½ teaspoons GF baking powder					
1½ teaspoons GF baking soda					
½ teaspoon salt					

If you want to modify a cupcake recipe not covered by the above three base cakes, or if you want to more exactly modify a specific cupcake recipe, the following general guidelines will be very useful.

REFINED-SUGAR-FREE BAKING

For each cup of granulated sugar the recipe calls for, use ⅔ cup light agave nectar and decrease the liquid ingredients by ¼ cup, OR use 1¼ cups brown rice syrup and decrease the liquid ingredients by ¼ cup.

EGG-FREE BAKING

We like to use a solution of ground flax meal in water as a replacement for eggs. The typical ratio of flax to water is 1:3, but we prefer 1:4. Use a fork to whisk 1 tablespoon of ground flax meal into 4 tablespoons of water for each egg being replaced. Replace whole eggs and egg whites equally: 4 whole eggs, 2 whole eggs and 2 egg whites, and 4 egg whites would all be replaced by 4 tablespoons (¼ cup) of ground flax meal in 16 tablespoons (1 cup) of water. (This rule applies to most cakes, but not to egg-leavened sponge cakes such as the Tiramisu and Hazelnutty Cupcakes. This rule also does not apply to frostings.)

DAIRY-FREE BAKING

This is a straightforward substitution. Substitute dairy-free milk (e.g. soy or almond) 1:1 for cow's milk, and substitute non-hydrogenated vegan shortening (e.g. Earth Balance Vegan Buttery Sticks) 1:1 for butter. For buttermilk cakes, you can create a faux buttermilk by making an acidified dairy-free milk. Whisk 1 tablespoon of distilled white vinegar into 1 cup of dairy-free milk. The acid from the vinegar "curdles" the proteins in the dairy-free milk, giving you a kind of dairy-free "buttermilk."

VEGAN BAKING

Simply combine the substitutions for egg-free and dairy-free baking.

metric conversion charts

BUTTER

1 stick salted butter	240 g
1 cup salted butter	480 g

FLOUR AND CORNSTARCH

1 cup Artisan Gluten-Free Flour Blend	124 g
$^{1}/_{4}$ cup cornstarch	35 g

SUGAR

1 cup white sugar	200 g
1 cup packed brown sugar	240 g
1 cup confectioners' sugar	110 g

SWEETENERS

1 cup pure maple syrup	280 g
1 cup molasses	240 g

FRUITS, VEGETABLES, AND HERBS

1 cup blueberries	110 g
1 pint blueberries	225 g
1 cup flaked, sweetened coconut	70 g

FRUITS, VEGETABLES, AND HERBS (Continued)

$1^{1}/_{2}$ cups fresh whole cranberries	170 g
$^{1}/_{4}$ cup mint, finely chopped	10 g
1 cup raisins	160 g
1 cup raspberries	115 g
1 pint raspberries	230 g
1 pint strawberries	300 g
1 quart strawberries, hulled and sliced	600 g

CHEESE

$^{1}/_{3}$ cup mascarpone cheese	75 g

SEEDS AND NUTS

2 cups blanched almonds	270 g
2 cups whole hazelnuts, shells removed	245 g
2 cups natural peanut butter	520 g
$2^{1}/_{2}$ cups chopped pecans	250 g
1 cup shelled unsalted pistachios	140 g
$^{1}/_{4}$ cup poppy seeds	45 g
1 cup chopped walnuts	100 g

COCOA AND CHOCOLATE

$^{1}/_{2}$ cup bittersweet chocolate chips or pieces	80 g
$^{1}/_{2}$ cup unsweetened cocoa powder	40 g

LIQUIDS

2 tablespoons	1 fl oz	30 ml
$^{1}/_{4}$ cup	1 fl oz	60 ml
$^{1}/_{3}$ cup	$2^{3}/_{4}$ fl oz	80 ml
$^{1}/_{2}$ cup	4 fl oz	125 ml
$^{3}/_{4}$ cup	6 fl oz	185 ml
1 cup	8 fl oz	250 ml

TEMPERATURES

110˚F	45˚C
140˚F	60˚C
240˚F	115˚C
300˚F	150˚C
350˚F	175˚C
365˚F	185˚C
375˚F	190˚C
400˚F	205˚C

acknowledgments

In certain ways, this cookbook felt like a déjà vu of sorts. When we began writing our first cookbook, *Artisanal Gluten-Free Cooking,* we had recently had a baby (our first daughter, Marin), Kelli was on maternity leave from her job in the hospitality industry, and we found ourselves developing and testing recipes while navigating newfound parenthood. This time around, everything had changed and yet nothing had changed. We once again had a baby (our second daughter, Charlotte), Kelli was on maternity leave from her job in the hospitality industry (for the second time), and we found ourselves developing and testing recipes while navigating parenthood (this time with two daughters under the age of two).

We'd be lying if we said there weren't times when we had frazzled nerves. We found mutual support in each other, however, and ultimately we wrote a cookbook we weren't just proud of but were genuinely excited about. That said, no cookbook is an island, including this one. We didn't do it alone.

Our thanks go out to Matthew Lore, Karen Giangreco, and the entire team at The Experiment Publishing. After working with us on our first cookbook, you had enough confidence in us to do it a second time around.

Sue Mann, our tireless copy editor, your attention to detail and hawkeye for consistency and the little things kept our manuscript on the straight and narrow.

Our thanks also go out to our agent, Jenni Ferrari-Adler, and everyone at Brick House Literary Agents. Ever our advocate, your continued support and insightful guidance never go unnoticed.

To our family and friends, who have little impetus other than our own dietary restrictions to be gluten-free, you continue not just to accommodate us but to make us feel an integral and natural part of every meal. Just as much so, your unwavering support and encouragement for our gluten-free cookbooks are deeply valued. Special thanks go out to Pete's mom, Georgann, and Kelli's mom, Linda, for the time you spent at our home babysitting the girls so we could better focus on recipe testing and cupcake photography when deadlines loomed.

To the readers of our blog, *No Gluten, No Problem,* you remind us why we work so hard on projects such as this: as members of the gluten-free community, we are part of something bigger than ourselves.

And to that broader gluten-free community, especially those who have reached out to us personally via e-mail in response to our first cookbook to tell us how that cookbook has positively impacted your life: We would not have been nearly as motivated to write this cookbook, our sophomore showing, if we hadn't felt—thanks to your feedback—that we'd made a positive difference with our freshman effort.

Finally, to our daughters, Charlotte and Marin:

Charlotte, you were Mom's constant baking companion. Seldom wanting to be set down, you desired to be in the middle of the kitchen action. Strapped to Mom's chest in a carrier, you were constantly grabbing mixing bowls, pushing your feet off the countertop, and otherwise showing us how eager you were to participate in the baking process. We hope your engagement and enthusiasm continue.

Marin, as your parents we must say this: Don't get used to this kind of lifestyle. Despite appearances to the contrary, it is not normal to be turning out dozens of cupcakes per day, to be eating cupcakes for dessert each day (often after lunch *and* dinner), or to have a fridge and freezer bursting with myriad flavors of cupcakes. On the plus side, this temporary change in our family diet has helped to get you back on the growth charts for body weight—solidly into the first percentile. We would have appreciated, however, more insightful feedback from your taste testing. Although you seemingly loved every version of every flavor we developed, that didn't exactly provide us with useful information.

And to you both: You made it difficult, in the best of ways, to write this cookbook, for—in the balance between spending time with you and spending time with cupcakes—it was a no-contest (no offense to our publisher). More than that, though, you inspired us to be our best selves, to demonstrate hard work and dedication, to follow our passion. All these qualities, we hope, are evident and embodied in this cookbook. We love you.

index

Note: Page numbers in *italics* refer to photos.

about the authors

Kelli and Peter Bronski are the husband-and-wife coauthor team behind *Artisanal Gluten-Free Cooking* (The Experiment, 2009) and the co-founders of the acclaimed blog, *No Gluten, No Problem* (http://noglutennoproblem.blogspot.com), which *Easy Eats: The Magazine for Gluten-Free Living* named one of the top three gluten-free blogs in a survey of more than 75 prominent gluten-free websites, and which *The Kitchn* included in its list of "10 Inspiring Blogs for Gluten-Free Food & Cooking," noting the couple's "thorough and lucid writing."

Kelli is a food and hospitality industry veteran, having graduated from Cornell University's prestigious School of Hotel Administration and having spent nearly a decade with Hilton.

Pete is an award-winning writer (www .peterbronski.com) whose work has appeared in some 75 magazines. He is the author of three books in addition to the couple's cookbooks and a spokesperson for the National Foundation for Celiac Awareness.

Pete and Kelli have been gluten-free since January 2007, when Pete was diagnosed with celiac disease. (Their two young daughters also have gluten sensitivities.) Together, Pete and Kelli have taught gluten-free cooking at venues such as Whole Foods and the Gluten-Free Culinary Summit. They have been featured in publications such as *Daily Camera* and *Edible Front Range* magazine, appeared on Denver's NBC television affiliate, and were interviewed on National Public Radio's *The Splendid Table*.

Their first cookbook, *Artisanal Gluten-Free Cooking* (www.artisanglutenfree.com), received wide praise, including a starred review from *Publishers Weekly* (an "outstanding volume" whose "impressive breadth and straightforward instructions make it an essential, horizon-broadening tool for those off gluten") and coverage in *Gluten-Free Living, Living Without* magazine, About.com, *Exceptional Parent,* the *Oregonian, and* the *Washington Post.*

They live in New York's Hudson Valley with their daughters, Marin and Charlotte.